UNVEIL YOUR GREATNESS

Also by Sudhamahi Regunathan

From This Birth to Another (2019)
Colours of Desire on the Canvas of Restraint: The Jaina Way (2015)

Translations of Acharya Mahapragya's Works

Rishabhayan: The Story of the First King (2015)
The Sun Will Rise Again (2010)
Why Meditate? (2005)
Sounds of Silence (2005)
The Quest for Truth: In the Context of Anekanta (2003)
Anekanta: The Third Eye (2002)
Call of Dawn (2001)
Thoughts at Sunrise (2000)

UNVEIL YOUR GREATNESS

ACHARYA MAHAPRAGYA

Collated and Translated by

SUDHAMAHI REGUNATHAN

HarperCollins *Publishers* India

First published in India by
HarperCollins *Publishers* 2020

Building 10, Tower A, 4th Floor, DLF Cyber City, Phase II,
Gurugram Haryana – 122002, India
www.harpercollins.co.in

2 4 6 8 10 9 7 5 3 1

P-ISBN: 978-93-5357-955-5
E-ISBN: 978-93-5357-956-2

Typeset in 11/14.2 Minion Pro at
Manipal Technologies Limited, Manipal

Printed and bound at
MicroPrints India, New Delhi

A forest lay at the edge of a city. A calf was restless to cross it. Not knowing the way across it ran helter-skelter, sometimes out of fear, sometimes in joy and sometimes blindly, till it finally reached the other side of the forest.

That evening a few travellers stopped in front of the forest. They wanted to cross it too. 'Let us follow the trodden path,' said one among them. And thinking that to be a wise suggestion, they all followed the criss-cross track made by the young animal, finally emerging on the other end of the forest after hours of meandering. Since then, all travellers have been following the same path.

The naïve calf had unknowingly become the pathfinder. No one tried to find a shorter route.

Contents

Part 2
On Jainism and Preksha Dhyan

Part 3

Introduction

Appana sachchamesejja: Seek your truth yourself.

My middle-school teacher used to tell me a story about a bird which dreamt of becoming the ruler of birds. The monarch, however, needed to have some merit: it should be able to fly high or should be able to sing or should look beautiful or have some such attribute. This bird had none of these qualities and so, my schoolteacher said, the bird should not have had the audacity to dream of the *impossible*. The bird was a crow and my teacher titled the story, 'The Vain Crow'.

One day, the crow found many different feathers along the riverside. She picked them up one by one and decorated herself with them. When she saw her reflection in the river, she thought she looked bewitching. That day as she flew around, all the birds noticed and admired her and she made her claim for the throne. And for a moment it seemed like she was winning. Till, my teacher would emphasize, a strong gust of wind blew and the feathers stuck on the crow's back fell off.

She was exposed! All the other birds laughed at her and the crow felt very embarrassed.

The moral of this story was that one should not dream of power and greatness. One should just do one's duty and if one was good at it, one stood a chance of finding mention in history. Generally, however, great people are those who are different; they are not like us, my teacher opined.

The manner in which my teacher presented the case also gave the feeling that to aspire for success and greatness was to pit oneself against others. You had to measure up, you had to be *better* than them. So it was a kind of war, always in progress.

At that time I did not know that the crow was one of the most intelligent of birds. I also did not know that the crow is the only bird which never eats alone, it always calls all its friends to share the meal it finds. But most importantly, I did not know that the crow could have worked on her intellect and become a ruler on the basis of these two major qualities of hers. That is what Acharya Mahapragya taught me: your talent may not be the same as that of X or Y or Z, but you have some talent which is unique to you. Greatness is within you. He writes, 'Every individual has the potential to be great. As fire is instrumental in separating the essence of a perfume and spreading it, so too can right knowledge awaken the latent tendencies in a person.'

Acharya Mahapragya also said that since the crow's talents existed within itself, it neither stood in combat with another nor did it derive its greatness from the position of another. So, to achieve success, one need not be in competition with anyone. It can be a collaboration. 'There is actually a place for everyone at the top,' he said. 'Everything depends on your abilities and qualifications.'

With strong determination and great enthusiasm, maintaining consonance with other beings in this world, one has just to unveil one's own greatness.

My middle-school teacher, in all fairness to her, had not been wrong. She had grown up, as I had, with the belief that to aspire for greatness or fame was a sign of pride and vanity. We believed Mark Antony's rhetoric that ambition is made of 'sterner stuff'.

Many smaller myths attached themselves to both the pulls. It is often believed that to get to the top, one needs, in addition to qualifications, a certain measure of self-interest so powerful that it could be read as selfishness. It is also argued that if one desires to get to the top, it shows that the person is attached to a disproportionate desire for honour and recognition.

A discordance was thus built into the psyche: an opposing pull between the self-fuelled and forceful power of ambition and the restraining hands of 'higher' aspirations for an egoless state, a hiding of the self in modesty; the contradiction between what we want to be and what we think, or are told, we *should* be.

When Acharya Mahapragya made me relook at ambition, he described it in terms of discovering my true potential. It was a great booster to think I belonged to the category of being 'born great'. To 'achieve greatness' was reinterpreted as allowing myself to bloom, to uncover and discover my innate worth.

The process brought some revelations. For example, according to Acharya Mahapragya, desire is an expression of one's inadequacies. My little desire for a cup of coffee? A craving of the body for caffeine, came the reply. The coffee leads to other things, like choosing the brand of coffee, frequenting coffee shops, some eats, maybe a hot cinnamon roll and so on. Desire does not stop with one thing, and often leads to unbridled desire.

My desire for appreciation from my readers? My own lack of a sense of self-worth. This creates dependence on appreciation to feel confident and, of course, criticisms cause heartbreak. Our sense of self-worth is not coming from within us but from the opinions of others and so this desire for success too is the lack of confidence in ourselves.

Having confidence in oneself is not an egoistic expression. The difference is that the former is a true manifestation of the self while the latter is a false impression of the self. If that is difficult to differentiate all the time, Acharya Mahapragya gives two more pointers.

First, how independent are you? We are all dependent on so many people, factors, things. To get my cup of coffee, the coffee planter has to sow coffee seeds in his plantation. Someone who is an expert in plucking the seeds has to then bring them to the factory. The seeds would have to be dried and processed before reaching the retailer through the wholesaler. In addition to these first-level connections, there are also others, like the supplier of electricity, water and any other kinds of fuel, such as the food the plantations workers eat, and so on. This is called interdependence, says Acharya Mahapragya, and all life is connected through it. It is because of the bee that we have pollination. It is because of the sun that the lotus blooms.

This is different from dependence. Dependence is often one-way—my dependence on appreciation is an example. My dependence makes me react. With a compliment I get pleased and label the person as 'nice' and anybody who criticizes becomes 'horrible'. The opposite of dependence is independence. We are not and can never be totally independent. Some amount of dependence is inevitable; for example, an infant is completely dependent on her mother for the first few years. The question is, can we distinguish between the dependence that is inevitable and that which is not and try to live only with the former? The former is illustrative of confidence, the latter of ego. The former is indicative of action, the latter, of reaction.

That brings us to the second pointer to differentiate self-confidence from ego: reaction. How often and easily do you react? Reactions happen due to emotions. In these times of social distancing and lockdowns, even though emotions such as fear cloud our mind, we are facing less of our routine emotions, like hatred, jealousy and judgement, and suffering the consequences of our assessment with an inferiority or superiority complex, recovering from a rude word and so on. With emotional distancing, if we may call it so, we tend to be more calm. That which rocks our insides is our emotions. Acharya Mahapragya says our intellect is controlled by our mind, which is in the clutches of our emotions. So, we are happy or sad depending on the emotions that our surroundings have evoked in us. Acharya Mahapragya says the egoist reacts quickly and constantly to the outside world while the confident person is less easily provoked.

Acharya Mahapragya often repeated the story of Acharya Bhikshu, the founder of his sect, the Terapanth. One day Acharya Bhikshu was walking to seek alms when a passer-by stopped and said, 'Oh! My day is going to be so bad now that I have seen your inauspicious face early in the morning.'

Acharya Bhikshu is believed to have replied, 'Oh! What a pity! My day, sir, on the contrary, is going to be really great since I have beheld you early in the morning. May you live long and bless more and more people with your presence.'

The shamefaced man cringed.

Here is another story about the ego:

A lady had a beautiful bird, which would sing a melodious song early in the morning, just before sunrise. Like the cock which crows at sunrise, this little bird would also announce the rising sun.

The villagers loved the bird's song. The moment they heard it they would all jump out of bed with a smile, and start their daily chores. In those days, and in that village, they did not have alarm clocks to wake them up.

There was only one problem. The lady, whose bird it was, had a very bad temper. She saw the villagers spring into action after her bird sang and so would often threaten them by saying she would not let her bird sing if they didn't obey her. With this threat she made little boys run errands, housewives give her food and the men of the village get her groceries. She started living a very lazy life. And for all the help that people gave her, she was still very, very rude to them.

One day the lady had a fight with the villagers, and she left the village. She packed her meagre belongings and, taking the bird along, left, saying, 'Oh! You will regret it. When you come running to me and call me back, I will not return.' The villagers watched her leave with sorrow in their hearts.

She went to a neighbouring village. 'Now let me see what the villagers do,' she cackled. 'The sun will never rise on the village because my bird will never sing it awake.'

And so, with a false feeling of importance, she thought the old village would be plunged into darkness. She kept waiting for the villagers to come and invite her back. Maybe she is still waiting.

To subdue reaction and calm the mind has been an age-old quest. Some choose to be inebriated and feel that momentary calm helps them tide over the day or an incident or helps them to remain in a state of general satisfaction. That it may lead to other health issues is a matter that does not confront the one in deep angst and sitting at a bar. Some choose to give up the world and seek solace as ascetics. Perhaps they find it. Most of us live between these worlds. To us, Acharya Mahapragya suggests meditation to calm the mind. He says that to achieve anything one has to awaken one's energies. There are three forms of energies: physical, mental and emotional. To awaken them he advocated Preksha Dhyan, a system of meditation. Preksha meditation is undoubtedly a journey towards spiritual fulfilment but it also takes you through fulfilment in many other ways en route, including the material. He recognizes that meditation is a very powerful and demanding process and the best that a beginner can hope for initially is concentration of the mind for a few seconds or, at best, one minute. But slowly and with continual practice one can reach higher stages of meditation.

He understands that everyone may not have the aptitude for meditation. If you are not inclined to cultivate the meditative attitude, a small beginning can be made with autosuggestion and visualization. The mind can be made to think the suggested reality is the actual reality and that way its responses can be controlled. When you face your preferred situation, your emotions become conducive and that makes you respond positively. That could become a habit and, as you improve with your concentration, you will gradually find yourself meditating.

For those who wish to sit on a couch and argue their way to mental peace, Acharya Mahapragya suggests the concept of anekanta. Anekanta is a Jaina principle which asserts that truth is multidimensional and relative. Absolute truth is beyond the ken for most except the Enlightened ones. Most of us see only one aspect of truth. We do not see the whole picture. Anekanta says, truth is relative, opposites coexist and *parasparo upagraho jivanam*, that is, a symbiotic relationship exists between all living beings which says peaceful coexistence is built into the very definition of our being. Struggle and conflict arise only when this is not understood. Anekanta is a philosophical concept, established by Mahavira, the twenty-fourth Tirthankara in the Jaina tradition. He said all matter has three aspects: creation, origination and destruction. For example, new cells in our body are constantly coming into being. At the same time, some old cells are dying. And yet I, as an individual entity, am living continually. In philosophical terms, it means the soul is eternal, while the physical body goes through creation and destruction.

The philosophical concept extends itself as a road map for harmonious living and conduct based on rectitude. Acharya Mahapragya has explored its many meanings in his writings, both in poems and prose. A telling one is—

This is wisdom
Sun and shade
Always together
Yet never one.

Acharya Mahapragya believes the idea of anekanta has been his greatest blessing, for it allows him to see every problem from all angles. Anekanta makes an interesting observation: opposites coexist, like the sun and shade, like creation and destruction. If opposites coexist, then it could also mean your view which is opposing mine can also coexist?

Truth differs because perspectives differ. There is a story of a king who was disturbed in his sleep because some religious philosophers were arguing on the streets. He enquired what the matter was as he looked out of the window. There were men of great dignity and learning engaged in an animated discussion. Some had raised their voices. Some looked very angry. They did not even see the king glaring at them.

They were discussing whose religion was better and each thought it was his. The irritated king got all of them arrested and imprisoned them. 'You will stay in this dreary, dark dungeon,' he declared, 'till you all arrive at one common form of religion.'

So the religious men sat looking at each other, each wondering how to make the others see sense and agree that his religion was the best.

A great seer also lived in the same town. Hearing of the events that had come to pass, he sought an appointment with the king. 'Blessed sire, I am at your service,' declared the king.

'Son and lord of the kingdom, you are a wise king. I am going back to my master and thought I would take from you a concise description of your town so that I can describe it well.'

The king was pleased. 'Sire, I have eighty-four palaces and eighty-four marketplaces, with each market having twenty-four types of shops ...'

As the king droned on about his kingdom, the monk interrupted and said, 'But, King, why so many different shops? Bring them all together as one. That would be wise.'

'O learned sire, how can that be? Just imagine how crowded a single shop would be if it were the only one. And then people have different tastes and desires, how can one shop satisfy all of them? Being an ascetic, you are not able to visualize those problems.'

'Exactly what I want to say, O King. You are an administrator and are not able to understand the subtle differences between different philosophies. When you cannot bring into one shop products of the same kind, how can you gather the aspirations of many different types of people into one religion?'

The king then saw his mistake and allowed freedom of expression and faith in his realm.

Acharya Mahapragya writes:

'I have also read the other religions alongside and because I am a follower of anekanta I do not have a sense of being separate from other religions. Truth is truth, whichever philosophy has uncovered it in whichever way. This is the realization that was born and so before me philosophy remains philosophy and truth, truth. All other differentiations have disappeared.'

Neither beliefs nor caste nor religion makes one person the enemy of another. We could hold different opinions and still live together. We are not competitors, we are collaborators, and we can coexist peacefully.

This understanding subdues reaction too. It shows that relative to a certain condition, something may be good or bad, and thus tempers emotions. Reaction binds you to the vagaries of the moods of the people around you. An angry man says something, you retaliate, and he cannot let that go—sometimes this can even lead to war. Dependent as most of us are on external approval, we are slaves to others' opinions. Adverse comments cause angst. This disturbs our inner calm. It may even affect our physical and mental health.

Anekanta, in short, says there is more than one way of looking at anything, so there may be multiple truths.

For those who want to reason out with their mind to bring in inner calm, anekanta logically takes you there. It is like lightning that shows the path. The onus is on you to take that path.

For others who are willing to try out meditation, Acharya Mahapragya has a world of practices to offer. These practices are primarily to quieten and still the mind. The route he takes is through the emotions which influence the mind. The emotions in turn arise in the consciousness. To clear the consciousness of volatile emotions, Acharya Mahapragya leads you through meditation. The goal, he says, is to reach a state of thoughtlessness. That does not happen easily, he admits. With practice, it is possible. Knowledge has its limits. It is gained through intellectual pursuits or through experience. Both are limited. The state of thoughtlessness helps to grow one's intuition. Intuition can access that which does not fall within the realm of our knowledge or experience.

'Work on yourself,' says Acharya Mahapragya, 'without doubting yourself.'

A story is told of two young boys who found two large eggs of peacocks in a forest. Each took one home and kept it in a pen. One of the boys could not take his mind off it. He kept going back to pick up the egg and shake it and put it to his ear, hoping to hear something. The other boy let it be. He was sure a beautiful peacock or peahen would emerge out of it one day. He waited patiently for that day. Soon enough, the egg did hatch, and a chick did peaked through. The other boy had shaken the egg too much. It could never hatch. Doubt destroys. Do not doubt yourself.

Working on yourself will present a perfect you, a you who is great. Remove the veil that is masking your greatness.

Hand the lamp
Over to the Sun
Let it look at itself.

Sudhamahi Regunathan
6 April 2022
Delhi

Part 1

1
My Mantras to Success

Should one shy away from aspiring for resounding success? Should one be ashamed to say, 'I want people to see I am great?'

You are great. Each individual is great.

The world should see your greatness. Here are some truths that help to conquer the world in body and spirit. Finding a harmonious understanding of success and greatness is essential for dispelling the notion that it is not gracious to aspire for them. This chapter prepares you for the process of attaining them. A process that is more beneficial and rewarding than the end itself. This process is also called living and has been culled from deep philosophical thought.

Success and greatness are necessary for every person. Of course, each one of us may understand the terms 'success' and 'greatness' differently. Let us keep aside our individual understanding for now. I am sure we all agree that we should not move towards smallness or meanness. Every person should awaken to the resolve of achieving greatness, as he or she defines it, and move in that direction. It is not just about desiring greatness and success, but about achieving self-perfection. With self-perfection, greatness follows. So, I think, to want to be great is a good resolve and that the process of preparing oneself to achieve greatness is worth undergoing.

To unveil the secrets of success, I believe, one must understand the subtle world.

What is the subtle world? There are two worlds: the manifest and the unmanifest. For example, only a few hours ago, when it was still night and it was still dark, there were stars in the sky. But now they have all disappeared and the sun is shining bright. Which is the real world? That which we see now or that which is hidden now? What I can see in the light I cannot see in the dark. What I can see through a microscope, I cannot see with my naked eye. Similarly, there is a world which we see intuitively and sometimes experience—that is the subtle world. It is far more expansive than our manifested world. Most of our daily interactions and understanding of the world are based on what we can see—that which is visible. The unmanifested world is the subtle world.

Till we move away from the gross and enter the subtle world, only superficial things will strike us and not the finer details.

I speak from my experience of almost ninety years, of which eighty years have been lived as a monk.

What I hold as my successes

Perhaps what I define as my greatest success is that I have never been reprimanded for lack of wisdom. Under no circumstance was I ever told, 'Be wise, this is not right.'

There are three stages to a person's development: the development of the mind, the development of the intellect and the development of wisdom. The mind thinks. The intellect decides. Wisdom chooses between the beneficial and the unworthy. Intellect is beyond the mind and wisdom beyond the intellect.

With wisdom, intuition develops. I have experienced times when, with my extra-sensory powers, I have learnt certain truths. I believe it is possible for each of us to develop these abilities. In fact, I believe all of us have our moments of intuition. It is just that we do not develop it so that such moments occur often and over a longer duration. I also believe that the measure of success should be as great as the greatness one is setting out to achieve. In other words, getting a promotion or buying a big house do not count as my measures of success; they could, at best, be milestones along our journey towards success.

Three pointers to success

That person can make his life a success whose life has purity, utility and momentum.

One midsummer morning, a group of men and women travelling on foot felt very thirsty. The sun was directly above, and its rays were relentless. They looked around for water to quench their thirst. After about half an hour's search, they heard a waterfall and headed in that direction.

Sure enough, they came upon a waterfall, gushing and gurgling down in cascades. One of the travellers stepped forward and cupped his hands to drink the water when his eyes fell on a board that said, 'Accept me as your ideal.'

Now, instead of drinking the water they had come searching for, the weary travellers began discussing how a waterfall could be held as an ideal.

One of them said, 'I know why. The waterfall is *gatishil* or represents constant movement or progress. To do so, it is continuously at work exerting itself. A lazy person cannot do this. That which incorporates pace or *gati* into its very being is worthy of being held as an ideal.'

Everybody agreed and looked at the hurrying waters with new respect.

'I think there is yet another dimension,' said the second person rubbing her chin thoughtfully. 'One who is of use to others can also be held as an ideal. The water quenches everybody's thirst: it neither discriminates nor charges any price. The cool water must be giving relief to many weary travellers. Where there is usefulness, a vision of the ideal can be seen.'

The travellers got so excited about the attributes of the waterfall that they forgot their thirst.

A third person said, 'I entirely agree with you, but would like to add to it. The waterfall is useful because it has pure water or else nobody would drink of it. Its purity makes it worth holding up as an ideal.'

We must move in the direction of the waterfall. When anything is no longer useful, it is forgotten. Take a simple example. When summer arrives, we put away our woollens. They lie locked up in cupboards, trunks and boxes. That which is not of use is put away. Therefore, one should be of use to one's immediate surroundings and to society as a whole. One can be useful only when one bears no ill will and does not harbour negative energies.

The waterfall is our teacher in this story. A teacher not only teaches the subject but also takes the disciple along the path of right conduct. When we say purity, we mean right conduct. My favourite sutra is a phrase in Prakrit: *Asisassa natthi sisa*—meaning a good pupil can become a teacher and have pupils because he has learnt to be disciplined, obedient and repose faith in the teacher. The one who has never been a good student or never abided by any discipline will never have the capability to be a guru. *Natthi sisa asisassa*—the one without a teacher has no disciples. Humility, discipline and faith bring purity to mind and character. These qualities help in the sublimation of our emotions and our desires. To be emotionally balanced leads to purity within and right conduct.

Along with purity, one must develop usefulness. A selfish person cannot be useful. I was initiated into the culture of being useful because my guru was always useful to people. I did not learn it consciously, it just got absorbed into my life and continued to grow.

One must remember, only that person who is healthy can be useful to others. Good health means having a healthy body and a happy mind.

Hard work is essential for any kind of development. So, like the waterfall, we should be constantly moving. That does not mean physically alone, but also intellectually. We should be continually learning. Since childhood I had 'rebellious' ideas. I liked change. It was thrilling. When I read socialist and communist literature, including the works of Marx, Lenin,

Engels and other thinkers, my leanings towards rebellion only grew further. Rebellion, here, means questioning established ways and attitudes, examining inequalities with indignation and so on. The attitude of rebellion makes one think. When combined with the qualities of purity and utility, it becomes a process of self-refining. It makes one rethink and hone one's beliefs constantly. Therefore, I have believed in growing constantly. If I look at my life as a monk, and subtract some years while I was gathering knowledge, the rest can be described as constantly upgrading my views and gaining momentum in my thoughts.

A coming together of these things is what I call success.

I want to unveil and establish that truth, based on which every person can build his or her life. It can be useful for oneself as well as for others.

2

Strategize for Success

Of course, one must have a strategy in place to achieve anything, particularly if it is to achieve success and greatness by maximizing potential. To plan out the strategy, the first step is to understand how to think. It is fashionable to say, 'Think positively,' but what does positive thinking entail? Are there some steps we could follow to make our mind think positively?

We begin by wondering, how much of us is defined by our thinking? What is the purpose of thought? How to think, constructively and positively?

The French philosopher Rene Descartes famously said, 'I think, therefore I am. That "I think" proves that "I exist"—I exist because I think.'

If I were to put it in dialectical terms, I would say, 'I exist and since I possess a developed brain, therefore I think.' My contention is that we do not think because we are, but because we are; and because we are in possession of a brain that is capable of functioning at many levels, we think.

Thinking does not characterize the brain; it is only a function and hence cannot be a feature. Our existence and consciousness transcend thought. Thinking is merely a spark of light, not the entire flame. Freedom from thought is total illumination.

What is the path to total illumination?

There are two states to be in: the thoughtless state and the thinking state. The state of thoughtlessness lies beyond the realm of thoughts. We can transcend thoughts through meditation for we will then enter a state of direct experience. In the presence of direct experience, thought loses its *raison d'etre* and comes to an end spontaneously. Everything is apparent, and this becomes crystal clear because there is no process of cognition. We see things as they are. There is no necessity for thought whatsoever. Where there is direct cognition, there is no need for thinking. Where there is thought, there can be no perception.

There are three ways of experiencing: through knowing, through seeing and through thinking.

Someone asked, 'Has your assistant performed the task assigned to him?'

The boss replied, 'I do not know, I will find out and tell you.'

In this case, thinking is not necessary for it refers to an action performed or not performed by someone else. One just has to report what one finds out.

In another case a person asked another, 'Have you got such-and-such article in your house?' Here, too there was no room for thought. The first question elicited the answer, 'I will find out.' The second question elicited the answer, 'I will see.' To find out and to see do not call for thinking in its true sense. That which is hidden, not evident, about which it is not possible to say anything with certainty, necessitates thought.

Thinking is a function of the cerebral consciousness. It is thus a mere ray of light, not total illumination. As one progresses towards thoughtlessness, the level of perception begins to grow. When, in the clarity of perception, one attains direct vision, all thought stands transcended.

The object of *dhyana sadhana* or the practice of meditation is to enter the subtle world and achieve direct experience. When there is direct experience, thinking comes to an end and knowledge, in its wholeness, is born.

All this discussion on thoughtlessness is valuable because, ultimately, we do want to get there. However, as long as the individual is bound to the body, as long as he is tied to the cerebral consciousness that occupies his being wholly, and until transcendental consciousness is awakened in him thought has its utility and it is not possible to do away with it altogether.

Two kinds of people are free from thinking. One who has attained direct perception and the second who is a blockhead. The enlightened one does not think because he or she perceives clearly what is. The foolish person does not know how to think; he/she is incapable of thought.

Thus, two kinds of people enjoy freedom from thinking: the enlightened one and the ignoramus. What a contradiction and yet such contradictions are found time and again. Only two kinds of people are unmoved by disgrace or honour: the wise one and the foolish one. In a person freed from all passions, all disparities cease; his whole disposition changes. The foolish person cannot tell the difference between honour and disgrace. So, for entirely different reasons, these two remain unaffected by the external environment.

It may seem paradoxical that at one level I extol the need for thought and at another I advocate the practice of meditation to be free from thought. The ultimate objective is to achieve complete freedom from thought. But let us be realistic. Such an achievement is not possible at this moment. It is an illusion to think one can reach the thoughtless state as soon as one begins meditation. If anything, during meditation, the flow of thoughts becomes all the more powerful. Even thoughts which ordinarily never enter the mind surface up during meditation. The moment a person assumes the posture of meditation or that of *kayotsarga* (relaxation with self-awareness), remote thoughts that seemed to have been long forgotten suddenly crowd back in his mind. Many beginners have thought of abandoning meditation for this very reason. The increased flow of thoughts is inevitable at that time when the mind is relaxed. When a person is stressed everything is loath to go near him, even thoughts! So as long as the state of meditation continues, these thoughts will keep coming up fearlessly!

Let not the practice of meditation be disturbed by such thoughts. One should, instead watch the thoughts. As perception matures, the flow of thought will be weakened by themselves. Similarly, with the awakening of consciousness, the capacity for direct experience would ripen and the flow of thought will become more and more feeble. It is unrealistic to expect thought to stop on the very first day of meditation.

While we wait for our meditative practice to grow and mature, we must learn how to think so that our thoughts support us.

Thinking is an art. Rarely does one come across a person who knows how to think. The person who knows how to think finds his life smooth and easy.

Lesson from a thief

An ascetic once said in the course of a discussion, 'I have certainly learnt something from every kind of person.'

'What about from a thief?' someone asked.

Replied the ascetic, 'Once I was staying in the house of a thief. Every night he would go out, and on his return, I would ask him what he got. He would say he got nothing but always added, "Tomorrow may be better." This went on for a month. And I reflected on how the thief losing his sleep still went out every night in the hope of finding something. So, from him I learnt never to despair in the path of devotion.'

Evil commands more commitment

Man's nature is indeed strange and incomprehensible. A person engaged in good work gets disappointed far too easily while the person engaged in evil work never loses hope.

This is a fact. After a great deal of thought I have come to the conclusion that evil commands much more commitment than goodness.

To be committed towards goodness one needs far greater and stronger devotion. It is the absence of faith that spells despair. Excitement and evil seem so bound together that a man takes to evil and his commitment therein is strengthened by itself. Not much effort is required in that direction. But to strengthen commitment along the path of goodness, tremendous effort is called for.

What is right thinking?

How are we to think rightly? It is essential to learn how to think, because a person with a negative approach will not be able to recognize the truth that comes his way for he will reject everything, while a person with a positive approach will access the truth and eventually find solutions to his problems.

There are two ways of thinking: positive and negative. These are the two ends of a spectrum. Most often we lie in between. There are combinations of the negative and the positive that lie all along the way. We are considering the extreme positions to make the understanding of the other combinations easier.

Much too often we indulge in destructive negative thinking which leads to despair, loss of enthusiasm, depression and the dereliction of duty and proactive action. In short, negative thinking means the beginning of failure in life.

The key to success lies in constructive positive thinking. Constructive thinking comes to that person, who, like the lesson taught by the gushing waterfall, keeps his mind focussed (constantly updating herself), heart pure (not sullied by overactive emotions) and practises detachment or attachment to all (is useful to one and all).

Constructive and destructive thinking have certain criteria by which we can identify them.

The first step is to examine if our vision is partial or whole, whether it is integrated or fragmented, because a person with holistic vision can think constructively and will get a balanced and comprehensive perspective, but a person with partial vision does not get things straight. In the absence of a holistic view of any given situation or incident, thinking based on a partial view or insufficient facts remains inadequate. So, a complete overall view is very important for right and balanced thinking. When the whole picture or a comprehensive view is before us, many conflicts get resolved automatically. It is because we have heard or read or decided to believe in only a part of the whole story that we keep getting entangled in labyrinthine problems.

Once a group of travellers halted for rest under the cool shade of a mango tree. One of them said, 'Along our way I saw a red lizard on a tree.' Another piped, 'Oh no! It was green. I saw it too.' Soon the discussion turned into an argument. It looked like they would come to blows when a third one said, 'Are you talking about the chameleon? I too saw it. It changes colour. So, both of you are right.'

The world we live in is much like a chameleon. Everything here changes from minute to minute, including we ourselves. How many different faces does a person wear in a day? Calm in the morning, hurried during the day, stressed at times, laughing at other times, in a rage occasionally and so on. Even in the ocean, tides rise and fall only twice in a day; once in the morning and once at night. In one day, however, our thoughts change a million times, some exuberant, some depressing. There is continual rise and fall. No constancy. No stability. Sometimes a person's behaviour may be rooted in some of his past experiences. So, one may require knowing a little about the person's past to be able to understand him completely. To understand and accept the different faces of the same person is to have holistic vision. There is little room for controversy in a holistic approach whereas a one-sided or partial view brings with it the possibilities of contention and conflict. The healthy approach to thinking is the constructive approach with a holistic point of view.

Emperor Shrenik's queen, Chelna was sleeping. It was wintertime and terribly cold. As she lay asleep, the following words escaped her lips, 'I wonder what he is doing now!' The emperor was awake. He heard these words which inflamed his whole being. He was proud of his queen's love for him. Now he thought, 'The queen whom I love so much is in love with someone else … Who is she talking about? Has she a secret lover?' His mind was in utter turmoil. He started imagining possibilities and built, in his mind, a distrust of his own queen and instantly developed an extreme hatred for her.

The morning found the emperor desolate and angry. He called his prime minister Abhay Kumar, who was also his son, and said, 'Burn this palace without delay! I'm going out to see Lord Mahavira.'

Abhay Kumar was stunned at the emperor's command. He thought, 'To burn the palace, to reduce Queen Chelna to ashes without any prior intimation—what sort of command is that!' On the one hand, there was his father's command; on the other, the most heinous crime of burning his own mother alive! He knew very well what consequences his disregard of the king's order would lead to. He found himself in a dilemma.

Emperor Shrenik reached the meeting place of Mahavira and paid his obeisance. In his discourse, Lord Mahavira discussed the topic of loving and devoted couples. 'Incidentally,' said Mahavira, 'Queen Chelna is the foremost among your queens. She is very pious and dedicated to truth.' The emperor could not believe his ears. He said to Mahavira, 'Respected sir, how is that? You say Queen Chelna loves me dearly. But only last night these words escaped her lips in sleep, "I wonder what he is doing now!" Do these words symbolize her love for me or quite the contrary?'

Lord Mahavira said, 'You know not the real meaning of these words. Queen Chelna came here yesterday to pay her obeisance. Afterwards on her way back to the palace she came across a Jaina ascetic who stood meditating under a tree. He was without any clothes. It was terribly cold. The queen did not stop there. [Bowing to him], she went on her way. While she slept at night, one of her hands lay outside the blanket. Because of the extreme cold, her hand was benumbed, and got so inert as if there were no life in it. The queen wanted to lift her hand but could not. Whereupon the queen exclaimed, "Oh, the hand was exposed to the cold for a little while, and see what has become of it! It has become almost dead, completely paralysed. Homage to the ascetic who meditates in the open without any clothes. I wonder what he is doing now!"'

The emperor was stupefied to hear [this]. He immediately took his leave. He thought, 'If the palace has been burnt in accordance with my order, a great injustice has been done.' He walked briskly. On the way he met Abhay Kumar and anxiously enquired, 'Did you carry out my order?'

'Yes sir.'

The emperor said, 'Abhay Kumar, a great injustice has been done.'

Abhay Kumar said, 'What do you mean?'

The emperor related the whole story.

Abhay Kumar said, 'Sir, don't you worry. I've kindled the fire, as per your command, but it would take a whole day for the fire to reach the palace.'

The emperor heaved a sigh of relief.

It would be apparent from this story how a moment of madness could have made the king commit a grave injustice. Many communal, social conflagrations arise from similar moments of madness. Impatience and impulsiveness can lead us to destruction. No individual should allow himself to be swayed by the momentary flare of emotions. It is very important to understand all the factors that make a situation.

Keep cool

Our brain cells constitute the basis of our life. As long as the brain cells are alive and active, a person does not die even if his heart stops beating. The brain is the fundamental seat, the fundamental basis of life. The cooler the brain the more wholesome one's life and the more constructive one's thinking. From this point of view, the second criterion for correct thinking is whether it is being done in a state of frenzy or in a state of tranquillity. Agitation makes thinking defective. Thinking is never balanced or constructive when the mind is in a turmoil. It can be constructive only when the mind is calm. Thinking must be based on facts for only factual thinking is of utility. When facts become secondary and only emotions govern thoughts, the thinking is never practical or sane. The thinking of a person who is not meditative, who has no control over his mind, whose mind is not balanced and calm, cannot be balanced. A person thinking rashly can influence another by making hasty decisions, expressing unwise desires and therefore instigating or taking impassioned actions, like King Shrenik was on the verge of doing.

Our thinking should thus be based on facts, must be reflective and not impulsive.

It is possible to change our selves and avoid confrontations resulting from impulsive, impassioned actions or reactions. That is why we need to enter the subtle world through meditation. Consciousness is ever pure. If we persevere in the practice of meditation, we will discover our pure consciousness. But that takes a long time. Whatever is non-existent at this moment should be taken as non-existent. What is only a future possibility must not be imposed upon the present, nor should a projection of the past be made upon the present. Most of the times, we are engaged in imposing upon the present either the past or a possible future. This creates innumerable difficulties.

When gold is purified through fire, it is a bright yellow in colour. However, if we see its ore, we would never be able to imagine such a brilliant metal lies at its core. So too can the lustre of the consciousness be encountered when put through the fire of meditation, burning away wrath, pride, cunning, deception, hypocrisy, greed, hatred, fear, envy, approbation and condemnation, like and dislike—consciousness riddled with such emotions is not accessible.

The inanimate world is free of such emotions—a wall does not react to your action of driving a nail through it nor does a chair object when you put your foot on it. In the inanimate world there is only that which is neither good nor bad. It is the animate world that is full of emotions that have been categorized as 'good' and 'bad'. The good and the bad are creations of the conscious mind. It is necessary to realize the conscious self so that awareness is awakened. Meditation is the tool to do so.

In this world there are some things which can be changed and some which cannot. All that is unchangeable and eternal must be left alone. Every state of mind is changeable. There is no state which is permanent. Anger, pride, greed, like, dislike are all changing emotions. Of course, the fundamental elements— sentience and insentience—remain constant. The state of mind changes constantly. When this truth is clearly understood many false impressions fall off. The dissolution of false impressions is the beginning of transformation. The consciousness transcends all conditioning. In this stage, matter is prized for its utility. Breathing is vital to life, food and water are necessary for its sustenance, and so are clothing and shelter. Their procurement becomes purely a matter of utility, without undue attachment. This new state of mind is cool and collected. In tranquillity, in the absence of excessive emotional excitement, creativity flourishes.

Having faith

Napoleon once said, 'The word "impossible" is not in my dictionary.' I think, today, the word 'faith' has no place in the modern dictionary. Distrust is one of the flaws in our thinking.

Faith has great significance in life. A life without faith has no foundation whatsoever. There can be no fulfilment in it.

Faith rests on three pillars: capacity, accomplishment and a knowledge of the universal laws.

Each person should have faith and must believe that he or she is endowed with limitless capacity. Each person should have faith in his or her power to accomplish any task undertaken. When faith falters, it is then that we find the commitment towards evil being strengthened and that towards goodness being full of doubts. Each person should also have a firm understanding of the laws that govern us and abide by them. For example, if a person says that he has full faith in himself and will not die, it is foolish because he has not kept in mind the rule of mortality that governs us.

Having an open mind

We must keep our mind open to new ideas and test them on the anvil of universal laws. Then perhaps new things can happen. For example, no one would have believed that man could fly till the aeroplane was discovered. But in the days before its invention, the principal of an American college is reported to have said to a parish priest, 'It is not far when man would fly high in the sky.' And the priest retorted, 'It's impossible! Nonsense!' Ironically, the two sons of the priest were the ones who flew the first aircraft. So, to deny a probability is a flaw. It is a closed mind that stands in the way of accepting something new.

A Jaina classic titled *Yoniprabhrit* records in detail all possible combinations and permutations of the animate and the inanimate in various forms of existence. In this text we also come across the possibility of creating all kinds of living beings. There is a mention of a person with magical powers having created a thousand buffaloes, another a thousand horses and so on. The story goes thus: A king knelt before his guru and said, 'Master, the enemy is advancing towards us. I am in no position to halt them or face them. You alone can do something.' The guru, it is said, felt bad for the king and from his knowledge of *Yoniprabhrit* threw some magical powder into a lake nearby from which a never-ending stream of horsemen started emerging.

Another story says a guru was teaching his disciples a technique of fish farming. A fisherman passing by heard it and tried it. He soon had a pond swarming with fish.

The idea of these examples is to say, do not discount anything outright. Keep an open mind. Of course, be rational but not to the extent of not trying out or letting a new experiment take place. Let there be space in your mind to say—perhaps.

3
My Principles

If one were to put down, as concrete steps, all that we touched upon in the previous chapter, they would go somewhat like the ideas that follow in this chapter. Embedded in philosophical principles, these ideas are realistic and practical. Some may sound demanding but when the ethos behind the idea is understood, the idea itself seems simple and natural. To be emotionally balanced, to have faith in oneself, to think in such a way that our thoughts help us, are all statements we may have heard before. The question that remains is how to get to that stage where we are able to harness all of these. Some of the principles that have guided me, I mention below, the foremost of which is the understanding of the concept of anekanta. Most of the other ideas follow from or are based on the principle of anekanta.

The perspective of anekanta

When I said we must get a holistic perspective of any matter before we reach any decision about it, I meant that we should examine its pros and cons with equal seriousness. This is called anekanta.

Should I think of it as my destiny or my luck that I was initiated into the Jaina tradition? I am asking this because anekanta is a concept that is specific to Jaina philosophy. Jainism gave me the anekantic perspective. I have lived anekanta. If I did not have the anekantic perspective, I would have got caught in one quicksand or another. Briefly speaking, the concept of anekanta recognizes that truth is relative and multidimensional. I will elaborate on this in the coming chapters.

That I got the anekantic perspective, I think, is my good luck. The one who is able to understand anekanta and look at the world through the anekantic perspective solves most of life's problems automatically.

A life of discipline

For the reader who may not know, there are two main divisions of the Jaina community. One is known as the Svetambara and the other as Digambara. The Svetambara munis, broadly speaking, are those clad in white, while the Digambaras wear only the sky, that is, they remain naked. Even within these two broad sections there are further divisions. I belong to the sect called Terapanth which falls under the Svetambara community. It was founded by Acharya Bhikshu (1726–1803). I consider it my good fortune being within the Terapanth fold because Acharya Bhikshu has given us a potent mantra—the mantra of discipline. This, in turn, has taught his followers the art of, and commitment to, discipline. One does not get to see this everywhere. I learnt to abide by discipline. I believe that the one who lives with discipline goes far in life. In the process of following discipline, he gains momentum.

Humility and self-discipline

The two sutras for achieving greatness are self-inspired discipline and humility. The one who wants to make a mark in whichever field he or she is engaged in should keep these two lessons in mind and live by them. The one who learns self-discipline and humility finds that success comes to him by itself. Discipline within an organization is what I have referred to in the previous paragraph. Now I speak of the discipline each individual must build within oneself for progress and development of the self.

I built my discipline. Without the need for supervision by superiors, one should control oneself. This kind of person holds the key to his own progress.

Discipline is the key to good health, and good health alone can allow a person to progress, whether it be along the material path or the spiritual path.

Everyone has something to teach

I read about Acharya Bhikshu and got an opportunity to understand the benchmarks of a well-lived life by reading about his commitment to restraint, sacrifice and penance. I tried to internalize his ability to forgive, his humility, his commitment to truth, and have tried to live my life accordingly.

As my field of study grew wider, I read the works of many stalwarts in the Jaina tradition. One sentence of Siddhasena

Diwakar attracted me greatly. The sentence that I read, learnt and embedded within my very being—*I have not come just to sing the songs of the past.* He meant by that statement that he is interested in building the present anew.

The sentence inspired me for it suggested to me that the possibility of doing something new always exists. Let us not limit life by saying everything is over and we cannot come up with something new, either in idea or even in execution. Some things are over, yes. But infinite possibilities are being thrown up continually. We have the opportunity to do something new every day. The desire to do something new also plays a role in inspiring one to keep learning and to develop one's thinking. You never know from where an idea will come. I too want to do something new. It wouldn't do to just sing the songs of the past. We have to do something in the present too.

My friend! Do not sing songs of the past alone, try to understand the present too.

I learnt from many people, not just those who belong to my tradition. The question of belonging to a certain tradition or community ceased to matter. I met and read about Vedic sanyasis. I will not discuss at length the influence they had on me but would like to report one single instance: Swami Vidyaranya was a professor of mathematics at Jadavpur University. He was one among the top eleven mathematicians of Asia and wrote a book on Vedic mathematics. It is published in the name of someone else, but it is said that he wrote it. He was very close to me and his stoicism impressed me greatly. Once he was visiting Jodhpur, Rajasthan, and I met him in the morning.

I asked him, 'Swamiji, have you had milk?'

He replied with a question, 'Where will milk come from?'

I said, 'So many professors follow you. If you just say the word, they will bring it for you. How can you be in want of anything?'

'Now I am in Jodhpur, and there are professors who will follow me. But when I go to Pushkar, I sit with the bhikshus (mendicants who seek alms) and get my food. Where will I get milk there? If I do not get milk, then my habit of drinking it will trouble me and I will crave it.'

I saw how a sanyasi is detached and free from the world. I met hundreds of Jainas and non-Jainas like him; Hindus and Muslims, Sikhs and Christians and from many other religions. I met many great men and women and learnt many valuable things from all of them.

Nothing is impossible

The main obstacle in the process of gaining success is despair. *It cannot be done*—this sentence is a great stumbling block along the path of success.

In my life, there came a time when my guru, Acharya Tulsi, wanted the Agamas, the sacred texts in the Jaina tradition, to be edited. It was a Herculean task. When my guru said that it had to be done, I said that it would be done. I have never refused to try. It was my sutra never to despair. Why should we think something cannot happen? When we believe that the soul has infinite potential, why should we think something will not happen? Keep away from despair.

A life of hard work

The second stumbling block in the path to success is laziness, or lack of effort. It can be done, but we do not do it. I have had some companions who had the ability to achieve their potential, but because they put in less than required effort, they did not find the success they desired. Can do but do not do—this is a great obstacle.

I have always believed in hard work. I have always tried to put in my best. My guru was a hard taskmaster. It is no small matter that I lived within the ambit of his strict discipline. I never shied away from putting in my best. Keep hard work in front of you, not destiny. Destiny will follow.

Constant alertness

The third deterrent to success is carelessness and negligence. *It is all right, it will be done, it does not matter*—these thoughts are a hindrance to success. We work a lot but are not able to safeguard or consolidate our effort. Our destiny also lets us down and success does not accrue to us.

These are the three stumbling blocks to success: despair, laziness and carelessness. I have always escaped them, kept them at bay. I have always thought that if I did not do so, I would not get where I want to get. So never despair, never be lazy, never seek comfort over work and never be inattentive to details.

Patience and waiting

I had resolved to always execute all my work with patience; hurry yields nothing. No work undertaken goes waste if you have patience within you. If you are impatient then the unripe fruits that your work yields will be sour. I understand fruition as not just stopping with the emergence of the fruit on the plant but in its ripening such that it is at its juicy best. A ripe mango tastes far sweeter than a raw one. Even if you ripen the mango artificially in the best possible manner, you do not achieve the same sweetness.

One of the most important secrets of success is to have patience, not lose it.

A young man asked Leo Tolstoy, 'How long to be patient? Can water ever hold in a sieve?'

Tolstoy replied, 'It will hold; be patient. When water turns into ice it will be held even within a sieve.'

Patience is a great mantra to success. I have seen that those who remained patient go far ahead in life. Those who were impatient and restless got left behind, lost.

Pleasant conduct

Another sutra for success is pleasant conduct. Do not let unpleasantness creep into your behaviour.

Pleasant conduct is a sutra to success. A person may be knowledgeable and wise, but if she is not good with people, she will not achieve anything. Pleasant conduct enables networks that are built on good relationships with people.

Do not think ill of others

When does a person's fate turn inimical? When she starts wishing others ill. No harm comes to the person about whom she thinks ill, but she herself is harmed. My resolve was not to ever think poorly of anybody. All through, over my nine decades, I do not think I have done or thought ill of anybody. Anekanta taught me to see things from the other's perspective.

Every person wishes that the other person speak the way she does, walk as she does, wear similar clothes, behave and live as she does. This is a universal desire. But that is not the way of life. There are contradictory tastes, natures, thoughts, temperaments and habits. Clashes are a result of this. Initially they are present in the form of seeds. Over time they grow into big wars. Despite living with many differences, can we live a life of harmony? To contain this constantly recurring question, anekanta has found a path. The path is of coexistence—the coexistence of opposites.

Sublimated emotions

It is necessary to keep one's emotions under control. Nine decades of my life are coming to a close and if someone were to ask me how many times I lost my temper, I would have to really think hard.

Do not let arrogance touch you. Do not resort to trickery or cheating. As a monk, it may not be significant that I was not greedy and had no attraction to material objects. However, I do believe that a person who seeks success has to bring his or her emotions under control, or else they will lead them down a slippery slope. A person has to keep greed away. Greed is different from aspiration. If you develop your capabilities and want to reach a goal, it is aspiration. If you do not have the skill or the capability, and do not work towards it either, yet still want to attain a lofty goal, whatever it is, a material acquisition or a mental state, it is greed.

Eloquent logic and strong dedication

Dedication and logic are the two wheels of life's chariot. Logic is very important. Without logic there is no way to search for the truth, but logic without dedication can be dangerous. I have developed a motto: do not use logic in day-to-day interactions/conduct. However, when it comes to principles or philosophy, I do not like to be second to anyone in logic. When it comes to interpersonal interaction, let the door to logic be closed. There can be no logical discussions there; only commitment to the relationship and humility work.

If you want success in life, do not be one-sided. Bring about a balance of logic and dedication by dividing the areas of life. When it comes to discussions about truth, let your logic dominate. When it comes to human interactions, let your dedication be dominant, let that eye be ever open.

Fix your goal

We have many short-term goals in our life. One goal should be at the nucleus of it all. Life has its ups and downs, be it a life of meditation or business or politics—no one is free of life's vagaries. But if we have a strong focus on our goal, if we remain dedicated to it then we will be able to overcome all hurdles and get where we want to. Identify your goal and decide where you want to get to.

My goal was to be a sincere monk, to serve and work for the Jaina community and the Bhikshu tradition. That remains my goal even today. There has been no change in the goal. Problems arise, difficulties come, there are ups and downs, but if the goal is fixed, we will get there. If we have not fixed a goal, we will get lost. A life without a goal does not get anywhere. I am happy to say that I have not moved away from the goal that I had wanted to attain.

To live and to die define our life. Living and dying are not anything new. But how long we live depends on us keeping in mind these sutras for success and our goals in view. Then our life can be useful to ourselves and to others.

Awakening of the third eye

That the third eye should open, should grow, was my desire. One meaning of awakening the third eye is to awaken the font of wisdom. Wisdom is our third eye. A Sanskrit poet has put it very beautifully: *ekaha hi chakshurmalam sahajo vivekaha*—wisdom is our third eye. Wisdom teaches us discretion.

Like and benefit are two words that often come together in Indian philosophy as *shreyas* and *preyas*. *Preyas* is that which is pleasant to experience but may not have good long-lasting effects. *Shreyas* may be a difficult route to follow but is of benefit to the practitioners and for others around them. She who gets entangled in the business of 'liking', or *preyas,* will rarely meet with wisdom. I have from the initial stages given preference to benefit, that is, *shreyas*. We cannot give up that which we like. Liking remains but we have to get our priorities right.

A wise mind will give twenty-five per cent importance to what is likeable and seventy-five per cent to that which is beneficial for her. Thus, the third eye or wisdom helps a person go far in life, towards that which is beneficial. On the path of *preyas*, there are problems and sorrows. *Preyas*, loosely defined, could be taken to mean attraction towards the material. Indulgences of various kinds come under this category. For those who love chocolates, to stop with one bite may be prudent, but not pleasant. The prudent aspect is called *shreyas* and the indulgence is called *preyas*. After eating a sizeable amount of chocolate, an aversion to it, a stomach ache or even indigestion may happen. That is why, in simplistic terms, it could be called *preyas*. *Preyas* is that which is not beneficial in the long run. Follow the path of that which is beneficial. The beneficial path is *shreyas*. In spiritual terms, it is also known as the path of dharma. But in day-to-day matters, it could be interpreted as actions which bring long-term benefits. For example, adopting some kind of discipline. There may be initial resistance to a lifestyle based on discipline. It may seem that it 'robs the fun' of many things. But, gradually, when the discipline bears fruit, like in the case of sportspersons, when strenuous practice brings rewards, then the wisdom in choosing the path of *shreyas* becomes apparent. The path of *shreyas* may thus not seem so inviting initially nor will be it easy, but eventually does yield long-lasting joy.

The second meaning of awakening the third eye is the development of equanimity. In day-to-day life there are many occasions for the raging of passions. Sometimes it can also manifest in hatred. These emotions cannot be avoided but the one who has developed equanimity will not be provoked by these emotions or get swayed by them. The one who practises equanimity will not try to like everybody; she will be liked by everyone. The person with equanimity is liked by all.

In spiritual terms, those who have volatile emotions feel heavy and old sooner. Friends become wary of their reactions and so do not much care to be with them. Those who have subdued their emotions are liked by all and remain young and light in their manner. People enjoy their company and want to be around them more.

I have found that the chances of getting balanced advice from a person who has equanimity are greater. I have also found that when you enter into discussion with a person who has equanimity, the discussion always results in clearing the head of confusion. But more importantly, I have found that when a person embodies equanimity, the person becomes very likeable to all.

The third meaning of the third eye is the unravelling of secrets. Even when as a child, if I got to know there was a secret or something hidden somewhere, I was always ready to investigate. It became my nature to unveil a secret or expose it. When I was about twenty years of age, I got a book of secrets. I still have that book with me and look at it periodically. It made me realize that the desire to unravel a secret is also called curiosity. Curiosity keeps one interested in the surroundings. Later in life, there were many opportunities to hear secrets. Searching for secrets remained a lifelong interest. After all, we have so much more to know about the world and life, not to mention our past lives and the future ones.

These are some of the principles which I think hold the secret to a successful life. It is true they are not born instantly. They require practice and conviction. For me, most of them stem directly or indirectly from philosophy. Perhaps with a better understanding of the different dimensions of these ideas and a sound philosophical basis, they may become easier to follow.

4
The Journey of the Mind

The first step is to understand your place in the scheme of things. Are you dependent? No? Totally independent?

Our life is an eclectic mix of dependence and independence. One leads to another.

To make a difference between dependence that is inevitable and dependence that is born of illusions and passions marks the beginning of this journey. When only the indispensable dependence remains, it is as close as one can get to independence.

Am I independent?

I am not at all surprised at not being independent. Not just me, anyone endowed with life is dependent. Vital breath is coursing through me. I am living. The fields are being harvested and I am partaking of the grains. It is raining and I am enjoying the waters, drinking it, using it in so many ways. My health and life are dependent on grain and water. Life means a willing acceptance of dependence.

I am seeing thanks to the light shed by the small earthen lamp in front of me. I accept my dependence on the earthen container, the oil, the wick, the air and the matchstick which lit the wick.

I am witness to a seed sprouting. The seed is accepting its dependence on the fertile soil, the water, the sun, the light and the air.

Is the lamp totally independent in bringing us light? Is the seed totally independent in the process of sprouting? No one is free from the hold of time, intrinsic nature, fate, destiny and effort. Therefore, no one is independent.

A parrot was in a cage. The door of the cage opened, and the parrot flew away. I asked myself, why did the naïve bird run away from its home to go to the forest? Why did it give up the readily available grains in the cage to feed on dry leaves in the forest?

Some unknown voice answered, 'The cage is bondage.' A parrot which is free to roam unhindered, in the vast infinite space, why would he be happy being confined to a cage? From this I drew my conclusions thus: the infinite merges with the void. So, when the void is itself caged within an enclosure, it becomes unacceptable.

How would water, which flows at the pace it wishes, accept the restrictions of a dam? A dam restrains it, rendering it helpless. Water recognizes the supremacy of motion; therefore, it is not able to accept stagnation.

And yet, dependence, and the binding that comes with it, is not without advantage. It gives power—sometimes beneficial, sometimes not. Electric current can create light only after being captured within a bulb. A bullet becomes more powerful only when it is fired from a barrel.

Water desires that no one restrain it
Grain desires that no one grind it
Wind desires that no one stop it
The mind desires that no one slight it
But water gives light when restrained
Grain gives taste when ground
Wind sends telegrams when stopped
The mind becomes edified by bowing.

We depend on language for our thoughts and communication. Our senses make us seek out good scents and sights and that inspires us towards progress and artistic development. Our hunger motivates us to earn a living.

Therefore, we have accepted dependence not out of folly or ignorance, but because it brings benefits.

However, bondage involves the coming together of indispensable or inevitable dependence and dispensable or optional dependence. And true independence comes when only indispensable dependence remains.

To see independence within dependence

If the self could have survived alone, it would not be dependent. A man with legs does not feel the need for crutches. So, dependence is relative. My imperfections decide how dependent I am.

The one who is independent is free from bondages, and is, therefore, lighter. But the one who is dependent is weighed down by the limitations of enslavement. In other words, bondages lead to attachment, making a person more encumbered. Detachment means being free of bondages, except for the inevitable ones, and that creates a lightness in one's life.

Once I was sitting in the midst of wild kidney bean plants. It was midday. The intense heat of the sun was making the bean pods pop. And I saw, to my amazement, the pods crack and the beans thrown up towards the sky scatter. They were bursting out of their shell with the joy of independence. This brought home to me the wisdom that the bean is willing to accept dependence on the pod till it ripens and that the pod is willing to let it go when it does ripen. The fruit is willing to accept its dependence on the branch till it has matured and the branch is willing to let go of it once it does.

That brought me back to my question: am I independent? I realized I am dependent only so I become independent.

Detachment?
A cloud that has
Moved on
After bursting.
Attachment?
The dust laden
Remainder
Slush.

5
Finding Freedom

Why is independence or the separation of inevitable dependence important?

When inevitable dependence alone remains, freedom from within is born. Freedom makes one independent, for then one does not just react, one acts. Reaction is dependence, action is independence. Non-violence is independence, violence is dependence.

With this freedom we recognize the interdependence we have with sentient and insentient beings of the world.

A well-known aphorism in Jaina texts is parasparopagraho jivanam—*we are all linked and of support to one another. Accept your dependence, and develop humility and camaraderie. Uncover your freedom, discover your independence therein and take responsibility for yourself.*

If the world were monistic, there would be only one reality. Then there would be no discussion on dependence and independence, since reality would only be one. But this world has many realities. They influence each other and have a cause-and-effect relationship. Secondly, every aspect of reality is changeable. Change is intrinsic to reality. Change occurs at every instant of time. It is natural for reality that is bound in the inevitable chain of changes to explore the ideas of dependence and independence. If some aspects are dependent, others are independent.

Independence versus freedom

Two schools of thinkers tried to define independence. The religious thinkers interpret independence as freedom from inner influences (passions which destroy the soul's attributes). Thinkers who have reflected upon the idea in terms of governance interpret it as freedom from external influences (imperfect organizational procedures).

Dharma is an exposition of the entire reality and its norms. So, its purview is not limited to man alone but to the organization of reality. Governance, on the other hand, has limited scope and deals with organizational norms, and so its bearing is on interpersonal relationships and the rule of law.

Indian seers and philosophers have concentrated primarily on a dharmic interpretation of independence. One reason for this could be that they did not want to mix the common and contextual changing rules of governance with the eternal rules of dharma. On the basis of their definition of dharmic, or eternal, independence, they tried to influence independence in governance but did not frame any separate guidelines for them. The authors of Smriti and Purana texts have, however, dealt with independence in the context of governance. They placed a lot of importance on intrinsic individual freedom.

Western philosophers have deliberated a great deal on the issue of governance and independence. Philosophers like Aristotle, John Locke, John Stuart Mill and others have established individual freedom as the base for independent governance. According to political thinkers, only that man is independent who does his duty—does only that which he ought to. His duty, or what he ought to be doing. is spelt out by societal beliefs or the rule of law. This means that without flouting the laws that govern a society or organization, man is free to do as he wishes. This freedom is used for social and economic growth.

In Mahavira's philosophy, the meaning of freedom is *kashaya-mukti*—freedom from anger, ego, disillusion and greed. Only a man free from passions can act independently. Insult for insult, anger for anger, ego against ego is a life of reaction. Any man who lives a life of reaction cannot live a life of independence.

A bird pecking at the mirror, a child trying to catch its own shadow, a lion roaring at its reflection in the well—all these reactions take place in the outer world.

The sparrow of the heart
Is pecking
At the mirror of life
And peeping
At the reflection
Believing it to be
Its opponent.

Freedom is an internal quality. The one who is free from inner passions looks for solutions within oneself, lives a life of action and is independent in the true sense. He is able to reply to insults with silence, anger with love and arrogance with humility, and faces assaults with calm. This is not inspired by the conduct of another person but is, instead, born out of his own internal thoughts, and so is any action.

Action and reaction: independence and dependence

The spiritual meaning of independence is action and that of dependence is reaction. Ahimsa (non-violence) is action. *Himsa* (violence) is reaction. Mahavira identified non-violence as dharma and violence as adharma. In other words, independence is dharma, and dependence is adharma.

In the inner world, man can be limitlessly independent while in the physical, action-oriented and social world he cannot be. In the outer world, the inner and outer influences curb his independence.

The world changes its own form. Its outer form is changed by the living beings, particularly human beings. Is man then capable of changing the world? Can she make it a better place to live in?

The answers to these questions come from two opposing streams of thought. One belongs to philosophers who argue for independence. According to them, man is free to do as he wishes. He can change the world. He can make it a better place. Some of them have placed great emphasis on binding action to time. Those who emphasize on nature, bind action to one's intrinsic nature. Those who place importance on destiny, bind action to it. Those who favour fate do so similarly. Finally, those who give preference to individual effort place emphasis on that.

Mahavira said that metaphysically, a real substance is that which has an intrinsic capacity for spontaneous action. It is not born out of any stimuli nor is it lost because of any stimuli. There are also some attributes of a real substance that lie outside it and are influenced by different levels of time, nature, destiny, effort and karma. When these forces are more powerful man may be dominated by them, even though he may be independent in thought. On the other hand, where the effort put in is greater, he exerts some independence, in spite of external factors. Look at it this way: Our world has changed a lot over the years. We ourselves have been witness to great advancements educationally, technologically, socially and so on. A human being is able to bring about these changes with effort. But if she were completely independent, she may have completely changed the laws of the universe to suit her.

As a person's knowledge grows, her capacity for work increases. Primitive humans were dependent on nature. Today's human being has learnt to harness much of nature to her advantage. So, her effort has played a vital role in disentangling her from what could have been binding or limiting circumstances.

Do you accept karma?

The common perception of the theory of karma has thrown the Indian mind into a state of fatalism, for it believes that everything happens due to karma. Everything is preordained by one's karma. And so, the initiative for individual effort has also gotten thwarted. Mahavira opined that *purushartha*, or human effort, could go a long way in affecting karmic results.

He believed that through *purushartha*, our fate (*niyati*), can be changed.

A king had to appoint his prime minister. He was wondering how to get the right person. Three candidates stood before him. He sent them into a room saying, 'Whichever one of you emerges from this locked room will be the prime minister.' The first candidate thought it was an impossible task and so did not try. The second thought he would bring more shame to himself if he even tried to do something as impossible as this. The third man thought there had to be a catch—after all, a king had placed this challenge, so he must have his reasons. He went to the door and pushed it. Lo and behold, it fell open. The king had not turned the key in the lock. He was testing which one of them would attempt to open the locked door and which of them would accept defeat without trying. To make an effort is life. Life without effort is no living at all.

Interdependence

Man is a sentient being. He is capable of desire, resolve and reflection. The first step of progress is to resolve and the second is to make effort in that direction. That is why man is the prime player in our quest for progress.

Feelings of joy and sorrow, and our principles, imagination, logic and sentiment have all been created by man himself. In the outer world he has created objects of necessities, comforts and luxuries. Man has created war and peace. Darwin established the idea that struggle is necessary for survival. This is eternal and universal, but not the entire truth. It is the prime cause of conflict among creatures. An echo of this is found in the Indian thought which says *jeevo jeevasya jeevanam*—the death of one creature becomes the reason for another's life, one animal is food for another and becomes its nutrition. Darwin saw the world through the perspective of struggle.

Mahavira saw the world through another perspective. He established the idea that the world of beings survives on interdependence. If there is the seed of conflict in man, why cannot there be a seed of interdependence?

The essence of Mahavira's teachings is that the relationship with other living creatures is not just one of struggle but also of interdependence. Each living being works very hard to establish and retain its existence on the planet and so we landed on the theories of survival of the fittest and natural selection. However, it is also true that without the bee, pollination would not take place; without the earthworm, the soil would not become fertile. Thus, there is also an element of interdependence between all living creatures.

Mahavira said that to establish peace in the world we should move away from the direction of struggle and towards that of interdependence or cooperation. In our lives there are fewer moments of struggle and many more moments of interdependence. Unfortunately, we are more aware of the struggles than the interdependence. Mahavira did not discount man's independence. He gave us the aphorism for a change of direction: man should direct his independence towards virtue and turn the negative into a positive. In other words, freedom from within should make a human being truly independent. The question remains: how does one achieve that?

6

Anekanta: Coexistence

How can opposites, dependence and independence, coexist? Learn the principle of anekanta—the practical perspective. Anekanta says that opposites can coexist. Not only is existence in pairs, they have to be opposing pairs. In the entire world of nature, in the entire universe of existence, opposing pairs exist together. If there is darkness, there is light. If there is wisdom, there is ignorance. If there is vision, there is the lack of it. If there is happiness, there is sadness too. Between these binaries lies the entire universe.

Can we also admit to the existence of consonance and dissonance, agreement and disagreement, similarities and differences? To admit differences is the essence of anekanta and the core of peaceful coexistence. Anekanta says truth is relative—can we, at two ends of a pole, both be true, be right?

What is anekanta?

This is wisdom
Sun and shade
Inseparable
Yet never one.

The desire to understand the truth has been man's eternal quest. What is its nature? Ever since man began to think, the question has turned rhetorical in his mind—What is truth? What is reality? *What is its nature?* The question has been posed a million times in our philosophical tradition.

Once, Mahavira's disciple, Gautama asked, 'What is truth?'

Mahavira replied, 'To be created is the essence and creation is the truth.'

A doubt crept into his mind. If to create were the truth, then creation would go on endlessly. There would be no stop. As we know it today, all that is created is also destroyed, but if that were not to happen? Population would multiply to such an extent that there would not even be space to walk. Due to lack of space, substances would merge into one another and there would be no space for any new creation. Desire would remain desire and would remain unfulfilled. How would new creations emerge?

So, not having understood the answer, Gautama asked again, 'Sire, what is truth?'

Mahavira replied, 'To be destroyed is the truth.'

Once again, his mind was filled with doubt. Creation is the truth. Destruction is also the truth? To be created and to be destroyed—how could two opposites be the same? Once born and then dead, what is left? The answer was confusing and he asked again, 'Sire, what is truth?'

Mahavira answered, 'To be eternal is the truth.'

To be created, destroyed and remain in existence is the truth. Truth is the conflict between the eternal and the impermanent. There is no absolute permanence or absolute impermanence. The eternal and the impermanent are conflicting opposites. This is the truth. In the world around us, if there had been only absolute permanence, then its nomenclature would not have been possible. How could it have been named? Since there is permanence, that is why we understand impermanence and similarly since there is impermanence, we understand permanence. But if there was only absolute permanence or impermanence, then their definitions would have been different. If there was only light and no darkness, then light could not have been defined.

The coexistence of opposites is a fundamental principle. It forms the grammar of all existence and of all truths, for if there were no opposites, there would be no truth. That there is truth means that there is an opposing truth also. The existence of consciousness is defined by the unconscious and the existence of the unconscious by the conscious. The unconscious without the conscious and the conscious without the unconscious cannot exist. It is compulsory for both to exist.

The rule of anekanta

Anekanta has one rule: the coexistence of opposites. Not only is existence in pairs, they have to be opposing pairs. In the entire world of nature, in the entire universe of existence, opposing pairs exist. If there is wisdom, there is ignorance. If there is vision, there is the lack of it. If there is happiness, there is sadness too. If there is consciousness, there is awakening. If there is death, there is life. There is the auspicious and the inauspicious. High and low. The disturbed and the undisturbed. There is gaining of strength and the losing of it. Opposing pairs define *karmashastra* or the philosophy of karma.

Our life is based on opposing pairs. If the opposition between pairs were to disappear, so would life. According to Hatha yoga, life is defined as the combination of exhalation and inhalation. There are five types of pranas. Of them one is prana and the other *apana*. Prana is the energy that flows in the frontal part of the body with its vibrations reaching the navel. *Apana* moves along the back of the body. As long as the opposing directions are maintained there is life. When this order is broken, life ends. The breaking of life or death means the expulsion of both these energies. When the two directional movements become one, life comes to an end.

Two centres

There are two centres in the body: the *gyan kendra* or the centre of wisdom and the *kama kendra* or the centre of passion. Both are opposites. The centre of passion weighs down the consciousness. The centre of wisdom raises the level of consciousness. One is upward moving and the other is downward moving. The up and down movement of the consciousness is in opposition to each other. Life balances on these two movements.

Opposing benefits

There was once a potter. He had two daughters. One was married into a family of farmers and the other into a family of potters. Both were happy. One day the potter went to meet his daughters who lived in the same village. The farmer's wife welcomed her father and in the course of conversation said, 'Father, our field needs rain. Please pray it rains tonight.'

When the potter met his second daughter, a potter's wife, she also greeted her father lovingly but said, 'Father we have several pots and left them out to dry. Please pray it does not rain tonight or else all of them will be destroyed and we will incur heavy losses.'

The potter was in a quandary. What should he pray for? He chose the path of peaceful coexistence: he told his daughters that whosoever's prayer is answered will share the income with the other family so that no one is left with nothing.

The world is full of opposing qualities. Each one's personal desires are different. That which is beneficial to a business tycoon is different from that which is beneficial to a daily-wage worker. There could be areas of conflict between those aspects which are beneficial to both. This is a conflict that will not end, though attempts are being made to resolve it. But then, how will it be resolved? This conflict is built into our very nature. There is no averaging out between two people's benefits.

Herein we find the seed for the idea that we wish everyone to be like us. We do not like the one who differs. We want others to dress like us, eat like us, see what we like, read what we like, behave like us in every way. To admit to differences is the essence of anekanta and the core of peaceful coexistence. To appreciate the talent of others and to accept one's weaknesses are also part of this learning.

There was once a man without a nose. People used to think of him as inauspicious. He was intelligent and so thought of something that would make the whole world nose-less. Then this discrimination based on the ideas of auspicious and inauspicious, good and bad omen, could finally come to an end.

One day he went to the market and looked upwards. People asked him what he was looking at.

He exclaimed, 'I can see God!'

The news spread and people began to gather around him in awe. But no one could see God.

The man said, 'I am able to see Him because I have no nose. Your nose is obstructing your vision. As long as your nose protrudes, you will not be able to behold this sight.'

There is never a shortage of fools in the world. One man went ahead and chopped off his nose, and bearing all the pain came to see the Lord.

'But I can still see nothing,' he said.

The nose-less man said, 'Hush! Say you can see God. People will respect you and thousands of men will cut off their noses and there will be more like us in the world.'

The man understood and exclaimed, 'Oh, what a lovely vision!' And so it went.

The whole world works like this. There is a universal desire for sameness. But contradictory temperaments and habits exist and clash, and conflicts occur because we do not recognize this. Initially they are just seeds, and then they grow big enough to cause wars.

Is this world only for wars? Will a person keep imposing her beliefs and likes on to others? Is there any third path other than these two? Is there any path on which we can live a conflict-free life despite living in a world of conflict? *In spite of our differences, can we live in unity?* To contain this constantly recurring question, anekanta has found a solution: the path of coexistence.

How can we coexist?

Coexistence is found in nature; to make and unmake, to do and undo. In our body there are a billion cells. Every second, innumerable cells are being destroyed and an equal number being created. This process is continual. To be born and to die. To be and not be. If the worn cells did not die and new cells were not created, the body would break. When both activities coexist, the body is able to function.

Life and death are contradictions and yet they come together and move parallelly. The same second in which a person is living, she is also dying. The same second that she is dying, she is also living. Life and death coexist. There is no definite time schedule for a man's life span. The second which is life-giving is also life-destroying in one aspect.

Thus, the existence of opposites is intrinsic to nature. Their coexistence is also intrinsic to nature. Nobody lays down the norms—they are natural and distinguishing. This dualistic world and the coexistence of opposites are nature's laws. Even the simultaneous presence of opposing beliefs, their coexistence, is nature's law. The first ever explanation of this rule was presented through anekanta. The basis of anekanta was formed by the observation that the nature of matter is such that opposing forces reside within it. How, then, can we look at matter from a unidimensional viewpoint? From a single viewpoint, how can we explain life or truth? It is then easily derived that like the nature of matter, we too approach truth from various perspectives.

7
Freedom from Reaction

In anekantic terms, action and reaction are opposites. They play a major role in our lives. Have you ever thought that by reacting to someone, you are actually losing your independence to that person? You are dependent on external approval. You hate adverse comments and are angry over them. Reaction comes from the violence bottled up within.

However, one should not confuse reaction with not adhering to discipline, not learning from another, or not taking good counsel. These are constructs of the ego which promote reaction out of a sense of false pride and arrogance.

Controlling reaction is a difficult but definite step towards non-violent behaviour. Violence is more than just the extreme acts of killing—it is encountered every day by us in small emotions. How dare he speak to me that way? Why does she look at my clothes like that? *The underlying cause for all this is that we want everyone to be like us, only then do we feel we have control over*

> *things. Ulcers and blood pressure are some of the results of the build-up of such emotions.*
>
> *To free oneself of reactions is to become more creative, more compassionate, more humble and, above all, more peaceful.*

Whether it is the new year, calendar-wise or beginning with my birthday, I always make one resolve: *Development and still greater development of non-violence in my life.*

I have often been asked: 'How is it that you have been able to write so many books?' or, 'How did you gain mastery over meditation?' I have one great maxim which has transformed and permeated my life: freedom from reaction.

There are two forms of violence: reaction and revenge. Killing too is violence, no doubt, but no man is obsessively thinking about killing every moment of his life. Nor does he commit murder every day. Hardened criminals are exceptions to this. Reaction and revenge are more commonly the seen forms of violence, and even between the two, reaction is more common.

During the course of a single day, we react a hundred times and a hundred times we commit violence. Occasions for reaction are never wanting in our life. One who is caught in reaction loses his creative power; he ends up using all his energy in destructive activities. How you utilize your energy is for you to determine. You can use it for constructive purposes or waste it in acts of destruction.

I made a strong resolve not to react. Most of the time I have been free of reaction. I do not harbour any malice towards anybody. If I found that someone intended to cause me harm, I told myself that person was wasting his energy. If one keeps one's morale high, one does not succumb to reaction.

The problem of violence is a formidable one. There are many occasions for committing violence in our life. But to not give in to the urge to react with violence, despite provocation, and to still maintain one's equilibrium and lead a life of action is a great achievement.

To lead an active life is to utilize to the fullest one's independent nature; it is to experience for oneself the joy of free uninhibited action. Whatever one does, one does with full awareness and responsibility and not out of any compulsion. The person who is reacting is forever a victim to another's will.

Here is a tale, generally told to children but containing wisdom for all of us.

A father and son were riding a horse. Passers-by commented, 'Oh, the poor horse! The heartless people are putting so much weight on it.' The father reacted immediately. He got down and, holding the reins, walked beside the horse, with his son still seated on it. A few steps later, they heard another comment from someone down the road, 'Oh, look at the heartless son, sitting on a horse while his poor father is walking.' The boy got down and the father rode the horse now. A little while later they heard another man say, 'Oh, what a cruel father! Makes his son trudge along while he himself is happily riding the horse.' Now the father also got down, and as the two were walking beside the animal they heard a group of people exclaim, 'Oh, how stupid! They have a healthy animal with them, they could ride the horse but instead both are walking.'

The person caught in reaction finds himself in a quandary. He knows not what to do. All ways are closed to him. His mind is restless, and he cannot decide on any one thing.

A young man had just been ordained as a monk. The new initiate lay down by a pond one day, using a brick for a pillow. When the women from a nearby village came to fetch water, one of them remarked, 'Look, he is supposed to have renounced home and hearth, but habits die hard. He still has a pillow under his head, even if the pillow is a brick.'

The young man was disturbed. He immediately shoved the brick away and lay flat. In the afternoon, the women came back and once again the same girl said, 'What a weak fellow, we commented on him using the brick and now he has moved it away.' The monk now felt maybe there was nothing wrong with using a pillow, and so pulled back the brick under his head. The puckish maiden was watching and said, 'What kind of a monk are you! You so readily submit to criticism or comments; you will not be able to do anything. Have you not taken to a monastic way of life? Why then? Let the world say what it will, but you must keep your counsel, or you will never be a true monk.'

To live in this world, blindly reacting to what others say is an impossible task. The great blessing of non-violence is to live in accordance with what is right, irrespective of worldly criticism. As long as the mind is caught in reaction, man cannot be said to be truly non-violent. Most of our understanding of non-violence is gross. Our understanding generally stops with thinking of the ant crushed accidentally under the foot as an act of violence. We do not see how reaction is also a violent act.

What is the cause for indiscipline? Nothing other than blind reaction. We are not ready to listen or are unwilling to accept what the other person says. Everyone wants to have his or her own way without any consideration towards another. To learn from someone else is no longer considered good—it is beneath our dignity to learn. The tendency to never accept what the other says, to flout discipline and tolerance—all of which constitute violence—are increasing day by day. There are two reasons for this: those privileged to speak know not what to say or how to say it, and those obliged to hear know not how to listen.

Discipline is essential for right living. Social life without discipline is a mockery—a lifeless pantomime. It is the power of breath that keeps people moving, that is all.

Discipline is the life breath to our being. Without non-violence, there can be no discipline. In fact, the greater the violence, the greater the indiscipline. Conversely, the more mature the spirit of non-violence, the more perfect the discipline. Non-violence manifests itself in an action-oriented life, in total freedom from reaction.

There is a tale of the monkey and the weaver bird in the *Panchatantra*.

The weaver bird sat in its nest on a tree and the monkey sat on a branch nearby. It was raining cats and dogs. The monkey was shivering.

Seeing him shiver, the sparrow said, 'Oh monkey! You resemble man very closely. You have hands and feet like him. You can do anything. Why don't you build a shelter for yourself?'

The monkey was enraged with this unsolicited advice. He destroyed the bird's nest and after dashing it to the ground said, 'Look at your audacity, telling me what to do! Do not preach to me. I do not want your sermons. If I cannot build a house with my hands, I can tear down another's house. That is enough!'

The weaver bird spoke out of concern for the monkey, but the monkey's ego (like man's) could not take it. The ego is the most poisonous serpent we nurture and nourish. That makes man look upon himself as the wisest and the best, a superior being who cannot be given advice.

With such pride in our hearts, it is impossible to develop sensitivity to non-violence. Will reaction ever lead us to freedom? This question is pertinent not just to a renunciate but to all men and women. To live in a society, it is desirable to curb one's ego. For a monk, it is necessary.

There's a famous story of Queen Victoria when she knocked at Prince Albert's door. 'Who is there?' came a voice. 'Empress Victoria,' the queen replied.

The door remained shut. She knocked again, and again the same question was asked: 'Who is there?'

'Your dear wife, Victoria.'

No sooner were the words out that the door flung open. For the empress there was no admission, but for the sweetheart there could be no bar. Arrogance begets arrogance while humility begets humility. The one great reason for reaction is pride, and when both parties are filled with self-importance the situation becomes an impasse.

Pointing out another's error invites a reactionary response. It is dangerous to tell a person he or she is wrong. Most of us would passionately resent such a charge. To point out a flaw in another is to turn him or her into a foe. This applies to everyone, including spiritual teachers. *Why should I try to transform someone and invite his enmity in the bargain?* Rarely can a man accept his mistake with grace. Instead of responding to criticism positively with, 'Thank you very much for pointing out my error. You have done me good. I will be more careful in the future.' man would more often react with, 'What do you think of yourself, you slip of a boy! I have lived longer and know much more. I will teach you a lesson.' A terrible reaction is born and soon changes into a desire for revenge and is ever destructive.

A man casually tells his friend that he is wrong and that sparks off such a reaction that the friend tells him, 'Actually you are the one who is wrong.' Imagining it to be an insult, the man reacts, and the feeling of revenge now burns within him.

Reaction is thus violence. The founder of the Terapanth community, to which I belong, was Acharya Bhikshu. I look upon his life as a model of non-violence. In my close surroundings, there have been two great apostles of non-violence: Acharya Bhikshu and Mahatma Gandhi. They have a lot in common.

A story about Acharya Bhikshu goes like this:

A devotee came to him and said, 'There is a man over there picking faults with you.'

Acharya Bhikshu replied, 'What is wrong with that? I became a monk simply to get rid of my imperfections. I am practising austerities to be free of my defects. That man is my great benefactor, since he is aiding me in my task of removing my imperfections. I am grateful to him.'

Somehow, we have gotten the idea that only if we hit back can we show our strength. Much greater strength is required to maintain equilibrium even under provocation. Reaction introduces violence, disequilibrium, tension and obstruction in our circulatory system, and sometimes this blockage is so extreme that it causes haemorrhage. In fact, much of the increase in the ailments today may find their roots in psychological violence.

The doctrine of non-violence is not just a religious principle. It is the secret to harmonious living.

It has been observed that people participating in meditation camps often reduce their dependence on the medicines they have been prescribed. Their problems also seem to abate. Why? Many diseases are psychosomatic in nature. They originate from the mind, from the violence latent therein. Meditation helps dissolve all psychological tension and bring about freedom from reaction. Complete freedom from reaction may not be so easy to achieve but at least meditation increases the time taken before a reaction. This means the reaction is often not so impulsive or rash. Continuous practice helps one move towards freedom from reaction.

One of the principles of logic is that every effect has a cause and every cause an effect. Very often, we are not able to get to the cause. We get engaged in the superficial symptoms. Many join meditation camps when they get fed up with drugs and treatment. Even though antibiotics kill the infection, if that is the complaint, they also harm the healthy parts of the human body. The cause of the disease may not be just the infection or the complaint of the moment, it may trace back to some psychological pressure. With that pressure being eased, the complaint may have greater chances of being addressed, with a combination of medicine and meditation

Meditation has been found to help in a number of diseases, such as diabetes, ulcers, high blood pressure, even eczema. How? Simply because these diseases are, in large parts, psychological; they are rooted in mental tension. We have never seriously thought about the fact that subtle implications of violence affect us. We think only of its gross manifestations.

Jaina religion places great importance on non-violence; it is the foremost principle of the religion. Its practical application is Preksha Dhyan. An hour's practice of Preksha Dhyan is far more valuable than a thousand theoretical discussions. It helps in taming the strong emotions of likes and dislikes.

Once a man came to Acharya Tulsi and said he wanted to have a philosophical discussion with him.

'But why?' asked my guru.

After some time of probing, the man admitted why: 'I want to vanquish you.'

'Oh, if that is all, please consider me vanquished. Tell everyone you have defeated Acharya Tulsi in argument, and I will not contradict you.'

The man was taken aback. Over time he understood Acharya Tulsi and became his devout follower.

When we are free of reaction, there is no violence within us. It becomes difficult for others to provoke us and indulge in violence, even if they harbour the desire to do so. On the other hand, if my mind is full of violence, mere discussions on non-violence will not help. One way of establishing oneself firmly in non-violence is Preksha Dhyan, the system of meditation that I will elaborate later in this book.

When religion becomes impractical and conventional, divorced from direct experiences, it becomes a lifeless institution. What can help us is a living religion—a religion that will help us attain salvation, here and now. Not something which remains a mere promise after death. If there is salvation for man, it is here, in this moment. One who does not value the present will lose oneself in the illusion of heaven and salvation, and not be able to access them at all—like two parallel lines that never meet but travel together.

Religion should aim at reforming the present, bringing about a transformation in everyday living. A strange thing has come to pass: people who profess religion and live a life of pilgrimage, worship and rituals still indulge in activities such as fighting, being jealous and getting angry. Of what use is their faith if it cannot teach them love for all beings?

It is a vast subject. Non-violence is a peerless light. One needs to reflect on it at every level to discover its radiant flame. The man who has direct experiences of non-violence is filled with unlimited energy. In him is awakened the capacity to die, which constitutes in itself the greatest power that a man can know. The ultimate power wielded by rulers of the world is the power to kill, they can do no more. But the man who has awakened in himself the capacity to die can face all world powers with equanimity—he becomes invincible. Nothing can frighten or suppress him. Our hard-heartedness has created innumerable problems. Corruption, evil and lack of accountability originate from insensitivity. If a man were humane, there would be no ground for evil to flourish.

And this can happen only through the development of non-violence. India once witnessed this power and appreciated it fully, but in the Middle Ages a change occurred.

Compassion from the heart, from the deepest layers of the mind, is the first characteristic of a truly religious man. To call a ruthless man religious would be a mockery. Life is not built on the basis of small or big occurrences. It is built on the compassion that makes them happen, on the sense of equanimity that underlies them. Plants bloom when watered by the person who is caring, and those that are watered by an uncaring person often wilt. Then how can one miss this aspect in the context of developing an evolved person?

The practice of Preksha Dhyan is an effort to awaken compassion. The aim is to transform the consciousness so that we can establish amicable relationships with one and all, including the self.

8

Beginning of the Spiritual Journey

Having prepared the intellect, learnt to accommodate opposites and look at things from different perspectives, now lose it! It is time to awaken the inner wisdom.

Just as the old traditional lamp has given way to the electric bulb, resulting in the devaluation of the former, intellect will also lose all its value the day we become acquainted with the power of natural awareness. We are unaware of our state of natural awareness because we do not know how to travel inwards. And so, we think our intellect is great. When we travel inwards, we get in touch with ourselves, we establish harmony within ourselves.

My being

Every action has a reaction. If a thorn pricks our skin, our hands immediately reach out to remove it. The pricking of the thorn is action, our attempts to pull it out is our reaction.

Some reactions are natural and required. But we must guard ourselves from reactions that are harmful to us, which do not further our well-being.

It is natural for a person to get angry if insulted. But how does one hold back from spouting anger in return? In some situations, it may not be worth it. In others, it may be more effective if one responds calmly. This is a complex problem. Our brain has formed patterns and habits that lead us to react in a certain way, despite not wanting to.

Ancient preceptors laid down the rules for an ascetic's daily conduct. They say, in such and such situation, seek refuge in such and such maxim. It is valid to an extent for all people.

As I mentioned earlier, it may be natural to feel angry at an insult. A sound piece of advice holds us from falling into the reactive mode: whatever one says, in whatever way, however uncomplimentary and hard, lean into it; find out the truth or falsehood therein. *Am I really guilty of this? Is there any truth in what is being said?* If there is, anger is out of the question. Rather, one should say, 'The man is speaking the truth. I have been negligent. I have unwittingly committed a mistake. I must simply accept this. I will tell the person he is right and I am wrong.'

If what was said is not true, then one should say, 'What is said does not apply to me. Why should I be agitated for nothing?'

If carried into practice, this simple rule will go a long way in keeping peace.

In another context, if a man condemns somebody that person is peeved. If he praises him, the person is happy. Both pleasure and displeasure are reactions. And the mind is conditioned to react to pain and pleasure automatically. A little praise sets the face aglow; the slightest censure makes it crestfallen. Is it possible to avoid such extremes? It is rightly said, no one can become a thief if called so by another; no one becomes a saint if called so by another. One's conscience is the one which knows whether one is a thief or a saint.

If one has self-confidence, confidence in one's own capacity, another's opinion can do no harm. Generally, man does not want another to rise. Ironically, the older generation can also fall victim to this kind of behaviour: when parents or grandparents keep talking about their good times and the deterioration of the present, they destroy the confidence of the younger generation and their capabilities.

The conflict between the older and younger generations is age-old. The elders have established themselves and gained recognition. The young ones are yet to do so and so in their impatience to attain that recognition they weaken themselves. The older generation is resting on the laurels they achieved in the past and are reluctant to be generous to the aspiring youngsters, saying their value systems have changed. This is true in all fields of literature, medicine, religion or any other.

However, this is just a reminder to us that if we act on the basis of what others say, we will be plagued by complex, either inferiority or superiority. Succumb neither to praise nor to condemnation—do what you think is right. The truth about oneself can be discovered only by the self. Only you can know what is feasible in your circumstances. Only you must act.

In case of extreme provocation, anger or insult, another piece of advice comes in handy. One should tell oneself, 'That man is ignorant. I will not also become ignorant. I will keep my balance.' This is a good resolve. However, one must add that violence has been traditionally categorized into three categories: one that arises out of the need for survival, one that is indulged in for self-protection, and one that is planned and executed for neither of the first two reasons. It is the third category that is to be shunned at all times. The first is inevitable. The second has its limitations, in the sense that it may cause the victim to turn violent sometime.

Two brothers were fighting over their property. It was justly distributed between the two till all that remained were two rings. One was a diamond ring and the other a silver ring. Naturally, both of them wanted the diamond ring till the elder brother gave in and let the younger one have it. As time wore on, both brothers lost most of their riches. The elder had only the silver ring left. He looked at it carefully and read the words inscribed on it, 'This too shall pass.' It gave him confidence and he continued to work hard to regain his lost wealth. Eventually, he did just that. The younger looked at his diamond ring and sold it to salvage the day. Soon he spent that money too and fell into great sorrow. He did not have anyone or anything to boost his morale and put him back on the road again.

Rise and fall are natural, just like the rising and setting of the sun. The secret is to never let your spirits fall. Keeping your morale is more valuable than a diamond. Wisdom helps to maintain one's morale. Sound thinking awakens wisdom. Wisdom tells us that problems cannot be solved by getting excited or agitated, it needs a balanced approach. It is not a matter of mere intellect. The intellect is limited. We shall inevitably be caught in the cycle of tit for tat. The intellect tells us it is but right to pay back in the same coin, to return violence with violence so that your survival is not jeopardized. But wisdom functions at a level where the intellect can never reach.

Wisdom is insight, inner perception, its yardsticks are different. The criteria resorted to by the intellect are no longer valid. We must build on a different foundation with a different set of values.

Wisdom is introspective. It looks within, not outside. It is the awakening of our *darshan kendra*, the centre of intuition. As this centre is gradually awakened, as it becomes activated, wisdom begins to rise within. Ideas, conclusions and beliefs undergo a sea change. The whole world stands transformed.

Once, laid up with flu, I was lying on the ground. I was in a small house in a small village with open skies. My mind was free and unfettered. Right in front of me was a tree. Everything shone bright under the midday sun. I looked at the tree and then the sky. They seemed to portray contrasts. The tree seemed to have a much smaller existence as compared to the vast sky. Small but limitless. The sky is limitless both temporally and spatially. And in terms of time, the tree is limitless too. Not even an atom of the tree can be destroyed. It is bound by the philosophical principle that says:

Anything that exists in the present, would have existed in the past and will continue to do so in the future. Anything that did not exist in the past will not exist now or in the future.

The sky and the tree have absolutely no idea of their being or non-being and yet they are unhindered and limitless. If every single atom that exists will for ever be, then how can I doubt my existence? When even an atom cannot defy the universal principle of everlasting existence, how can I be an exception? A little more thinking made me wonder why it is that man alone should doubt his existence. He has a more developed consciousness than the tree and therefore entertains doubts about it; furthermore, his consciousness is not so developed as that of a yogi, an ascetic, and therefore he cannot understand its infiniteness. From both angles, he has lost out!

Some truths in this world are gross and some subtle. I understand the gross truth through gross means and the subtle truth through subtle means. But I have no way of understanding formless truths. A mango is here with me. I see it with my eyes. I can taste it with my tongue. I can smell it and touch it too. It is a gross truth. The atom is a subtle truth. I cannot directly see, smell, touch or taste it but with a microscope I am still able to see it.

Formless truth is so subtle that even microscopes do not help to see them. This is its greatest problem: how to prove its existence? Since these truths are formless, they do not fall within the ambit of the senses. Since they cannot be grasped by the senses they do not fall within the ambit of my knowledge. If my existence had been separate from me, I would have been able to describe it in words like many have. Innumerable people have written and spoken of their belief as being a part of the eternal with perishable bodies. I too would accept it as a belief but when it comes to wanting to experience formless truth and not just be content with believing it, the whole thing becomes less powerful.

The senses, the mind and the intellect are all means of indirect experience, whereas knowing means direct experience. Then I get frustrated searching for my own existence.

If my existence did not gleam through my senses, mind and intellect, I would have been frustrated. But my senses, mind and intellect go outwards, interact with the world and then return home. I am familiar with this process. However, I have no clue of how to go inwards. That is why I am not acquainted with my existence.

One day my guru told me to stop the flow of consciousness outwards and instead direct it within. That, of course, comes with a lot of practice of meditation. As soon as I did that, I found myself face to face with my essential being. There was no longer the duality of or conflict between my awareness of my existence and my being. It was integrated self-awareness as an objective truth, devoid of all subjectivity. It is in this context that I have questioned the competence of the intellect and have refused to accept its assertion of the oneness or difference between the soul and the body.

Prior to the above state, I used to engage in intellectual pursuits—discoveries made with the help of the intellect. Then there was a duality of being and its awareness. I was the researcher, and awareness was the subject of research. The intellect had created this division. As soon as I prevented the flow of awareness to pass through the intellect, my being and its awareness lost their duality.

A man had been deeply troubled for some time. Somebody told him to go meet a spiritual guru: 'He will make you feel at peace.' So, the man went and, bowing low, requested the well-known teacher to give him wisdom. The teacher was busy. He told him to go to a pond outside the village and ask the gold-coloured fish for wisdom. The man went and found the fish in the pond. He repeated his request.

The fish replied, 'Sure, I will teach you. But, first, I am thirsty. Please bring me a glass of water.'

'What a foolish fish you are,' exclaimed the man. 'Living in water, you ask me to get you water?'

'Why?' asked the fish. 'Is this not what you are doing too? The wisdom you seek is within you, yet you ask others for it.'

Just as the old traditional lamp has given way to the electric bulb, resulting in the devaluation of the former, intellect will also lose all its value the day we become acquainted with the power of natural awareness. We are unaware of the power of our consciousness and so are dazzled by the intellect. As soon as we get acquainted with our natural awareness, the intellect will lose its power.

Intellectualism has made the indirect appear direct, simply because the senses do not have the power of direct apprehension. They have limited powers of perception and that too outward-going. Objective truth can be experienced only through medium-neutral awareness. There the divisions of time disappear. There I just am. I am the same way in the past, present and future. I can see time change and I have established synchronicity with time. As time moves, I too acquire pace.

9
What Is Meditation?

The travel inwards is called meditation. To touch the core is to unleash tremendous energy when nothing remains impossible—that is meditation.

However, it is not possible to just sit down one day, close your eyes and declare you are going to meditate. It is not an activity dictated by the intellect. It is an action of the mind and beyond the mind. One has to prepare the mind, make it capable of meditating.

There are three states of mind from the point of view of meditation: avadhana, dharana *and* dhyana. *To even master the first stage of* avadhana *can bring enormous benefits.*

Meditation is a method of knowing—knowing every event. Not only the good events, know the bad ones too. Not only the liked but also the disliked events. When knowing *happens*, nothing is bad or good. Nothing is liked or disliked. Like–dislike, good–bad, beautiful–ugly, these are descriptors that are ascribed after experiencing an event. It has no links with the process of getting to know.

When man is just a knower, nothing is liked or disliked by him. Nothing is beautiful or ugly. Nothing gives happiness and nothing gives sadness. Event remains an event, mode remains a mode, and knowledge remains knowledge. Knowledge is not a modification of an object. Nor is the nature of knowledge the object to be known. The two are different. One is that which is to be studied and the other is knowledge itself. But our doubts have merged knowledge and the object of study. Knowledge takes the form in which the object appears.

Meditational practice is the practice of enlightenment. Man wants light. He never desires darkness. So he meditates for enlightenment. He wishes that the darkness within him is erased. As light enters, darkness is chased away.

The purpose of meditation is to bring about transformation. The one who comes to meditate does so to change. If the idea of change was not there, meditation would not seem so attractive. Man wants to change.

Man has many hindrances in his life. Anger, ego, fear and deceit are some of them. If we move closer to reality and observe the truth, we will find that invariably most of our sorrow is unreal, caused by our ignorance, thought processes and beliefs. We suffer them. If we enter the zone of truth or get closer to truth, most of our misery would disappear.

An angry man suffers and makes his family suffer with him. Is it possible to change this temperament?

> Wise man, understand, I say to you, this is the truth
> of experience

Where the feet have once stepped, they will not again in the same place,
This is the truth of the material world.
And shrinking, the shadow which looms so large now, will also disappear.
You weigh only with those measures whose base has swung away
You want to tie knots when times are unravelling them all the way
You agree or you do not, times have changed for sure
That which was very old in this world has once again come back as new
This bundle of beliefs you hold true, how long will you carry it along?
Without experiencing life, will you continue to parrot the same things?
You think these beliefs are ancient and so have difficulty giving them up.
The stairway to go up and to come down is not different
As many people as cry with these eyes, also laugh with them
The difference is only with the feet which ascend or descend
The difference is only in the blooming or withering of form
When nature changes, change of form is inevitable
Whatever happens in the world is one's own making
Your assessment and mine; the difference also follows the same process.

Our body, psyche and mind can change. Our rays of consciousness can change. Our subtlest variations of consciousness can change. Our aura can change. The energy of our body can change. The chemicals and the functioning of our body's nervous system can change. Hormones secreted by the glands also change. Everything can change if we wish it. Man thinks he cannot change. That habits can never change. This is false and ignorance impedes our development.

The job of meditational practice is to change this state: to understand the respective places of the object of study and of knowledge, to let knowledge remain in the mode of knowledge and object in the mode of object, to not let them overlap. Transformation of the mind is required only to maintain knowledge as knowledge and the object of study as the object of study, to keep an event as an event and the knower as a knower. It is not necessary to do anything more than this. Once this realization occurs, it is not necessary to meditate for long hours. It is only when you are able to know an event and not experience it that meditation brings results automatically. Then whatever you do, you are meditating, whether you are walking, eating, sleeping or speaking. There is no need for silence. Silence is a restraint on not speaking all the time. You are always in the meditative state.

Our basic nature is to know, to see. This does not happen in a day. It is not possible to achieve in a day. We should not think of the impossible as impossible. That which is not possible to do in one day should not be aspired for in that span of time.

When our awareness rises, our felicity for mindful acts (*bhavakriya*) improves, then the question of experience does not arise. Mindful action is an important rule of meditation. We should live in the present. We should know the modes of the present. We should not get caught in past and future modes. To know does not mean one does not make any effort. In reality, only the man who *knows* takes the right decisions and makes the right effort. The man stuck in the past or the future is unable to act on his present.

It is true that the man who gets carried away by the event invites sorrow. The man who meditates should know this. But if he is unable to, he should accept that his meditation has not been successful. If a man's behaviour, conduct and thoughts have not undergone change even after meditating then he should know that he has not even entered the meditation chamber. Meditation is said to be successful only when behaviour, conduct, thoughts and perspectives begin to change. The first thing that happens is that experience takes a back seat and knowing drives the vehicle.

To make the mind competent to meditate

To understand this more clearly, it may help to know that there are several strata of consciousness. The most gross stratum is that which is connected with the sense organs. The next is a subtle one connected with the mind. The third is still more subtle and connected with the intellect. The subtlest one after this is connected with the *adhyavasaya* or the unconscious mind. Besides these, there are several other strata which we have not been able to identify and define. We live through them at various levels.

The sense organs are at a gross level and so their functioning is clear to us. The mind is a very subtle organ and, therefore, in comparison to the senses, it is difficult to comprehend.

Meditation is an activity linked to the mind. The senses are not directly connected to the meditative process. Its first point of contact is with the mind. Meditation can be dangerous, for that which is beneficial has the power to be harmful too. There is no such thing in this world which is beneficial and not dangerous. Anything from which we have great expectations of benefit, also holds the potential for harm. So, we should understand that meditation can bring both benefits and problems. If we meditate without understanding the right way to do so, it can be dangerous. Meditation produces a special heat energy. If one is not able to tolerate that energy, one can even go mad. Therefore, meditation should be taken seriously and followed carefully. It is also not possible that you sit down to meditate today and end up meditating for an hour straightaway.

To be able to meditate for an hour, long hours of practice is required. If one is able to meditate for just about two minutes the first day, it is an achievement. If a person can be focussed unwaveringly for even two minutes, it is a good start. One will find that few people, even after years of practising meditation, are able to focus and be still for two minutes. It is no mean achievement to be able to keep all thoughts at bay and concentrate fully for a couple of minutes.

The mind, by its very nature, is fickle and restless. Innumerable currents of thoughts and ideas flow through it continually. We are generally unaware of them. We begin to be conscious of them when we try to concentrate on something. Only then do we realize the speed at which our thoughts flow, one to another, and how distracting they can be. We are still at the stage of *avadhana*.

In the language of yoga, the mind is described as existing in three states: paying attention or *avadhana*, concentration or *dharana* and meditation or *dhyana*. Mental activities pass through these three stages.

In *avadhana*, we try to focus our attention on a particular thought or object. When the sergeant calls for attention, his soldiers fall into position—that is the call given to the mind at the stage of *avadhana*.

Just as we can pay attention to an external object, we can also focus inwards. When the focus turns inwards, insight is awakened. Then the attention is not focussed on external objects but towards oneself, towards the inner being. In this state of being, insight and inner wisdom are awakened.

The second state of the mind is concentration, which is called *dharana* in yoga. This state is when we focus all our energies on that which has caught our attention. To harness the mind and stop it from wandering, to make it focus only on one object, is *dharana*. This stage precedes meditation. Patanjali has defined *dharana* as the state in which the mind is focussed on an object. To bind the mind for a continued period to any one part of the body or object is *dharana*.

The third state of the mind is meditation or *dhyana*. After *avadhana* comes *dharana*, and after *dharana* comes *dhyana*. The intense form of concentration is *dhyana* where the mind becomes still, stable. When this state lasts for some time it is called meditation.

I have thought about all the three stages. Meditation is the third stage. We have to begin with the practice of *avadhana*. The mind moves at high speed; it is by nature fickle. We are going in an entirely opposite direction of wanting to arrest its speed. It is easy to swim with the flow; even a boat moves quickly in the direction of the current. To move against the flow is difficult. Mahavira said:

Annusoyyapattiye bahujannammi padisoyaldwlekhannam
Padisoyameva appa dayavvow howkammennam

When the whole world is flowing with the current, it is difficult to flow against it. It is further said, '*annusowo sansaro padisowo tassa uttaro*', or to move with the flow is called life. This is restlessness, the absence of peace, the presence of misery. To move against the current is to move beyond the mind and this brings peace and stability. The act of meditation is to move against the current. To tame a restless and quick-paced mind, to quieten and still it, are all against the nature of the mind. This can show how difficult meditation is. So do not take it lightly.

It is true that from my true description of meditation some readers may get put off, not wanting to do something so strenuous. But I am not trying to scare anyone. That is not my intention, but I do not want to hide the truth with any kind of falsity. I do not want to give the impression that meditation is simple because I do not want the prior stages to be mistaken for meditation. I do not want the seeker to stop somewhere in the initial stages of concentration and think it is meditation. We meditate to break away from illusions of the mind and negligence. I would therefore not like us to deceive ourselves about the seriousness or intensity of meditation.

We have to understand meditation is not a quick fix. It is a long process and we have to undertake it with resolve and in a state of full preparedness.

Even reciting a mantra is similar. Just as a mantra can bring benefits, it can also cause great harm. Therefore, the practitioner has to first learn how to protect himself or herself from the negative effects of the mantra. This protective step is like a *kavach* or shield. No mantra recitation should be undertaken without preparing the *kavach*. For every part of the body, there are different shields—from the tip of the toe to the top of the head, shields are prepared for every part of the body and only then is a mantra recitation undertaken.

In ancient times soldiers wore armours of steel when they went to war to safeguard themselves. Similarly, a practitioner should safeguard against any harm with a *kavach* before undertaking the recitation of any mantra. Of course, this *kavach* is of a different kind and serves to ward off external influences.

So, before undertaking meditation one has to prepare the mind for it. This is the stage of *avadhana*, where you collect your thoughts. Since this is prerequisite for meditation, I am discussing it at length. Many exercises are undertaken to make the mind capable. Asanas make the physical body strong and flexible. Meditation does that to the mind. The backbone is by nature not flexible, but it is made so by asanas. *Avadhana* makes the mind capable and teaches mental skills.

The mind is quick to perceive external objects. We have to train it. There is a method for training it which is explained beautifully in the *Nandi Sutra*.

The first step of the training begins with the methods of *alpagrahi-bahugrahi*. In the *alpagrahi* stage, the mind catches something small and concentrates on it for a short time. In the *bahugrahi* stage, the objects of concentration are more and the scope wider, and the duration is also lengthened.

One of the objects of Preksha meditation (which we will be elaborated later) is one's own body or breath. At the behest of the instructor, the practitioner is prodded to feel the breath at the tip of the nose. He has to act like the sentry at the nostril, watching that which enters and that which exits. He has to watch his breath attentively.

In the *bahugrahi* stage, an additional instruction is given: move your mind inwards with the inhaled breath and outwards with the exhaled breath. In *alpagrahi*, the focus was at a specific point, at the tip of the nose. In the *bahugrahi* stage, the focus is on the entire process of exhaling and inhaling and therefore one watches right from the navel to the lungs—the mind has to encompass this entire field.

The *alpagrahi* and *bahugrahi* steps constitute a single unit of concentration. The next unit is again made up of a pair of *ekavidhagrahi* and *bahuvidhagrahi*. The former means to see and concentrate on a single class of objects while the latter means to see and concentrate on several classes of objects.

Upadhyay Yasovijaya was a man of erudition, an outstanding logician and a master of *avadhana*. Once a hundred brass cups were placed before him and each one struck with a rod to make music. Each cup emitted sound waves at different frequencies. Yasovijaya heard them with concentration. Then he was asked to close his eyes and one cup was struck. Yasovijaya could immediately tell which cup it was. This is an exhibition of the skill of grasping sound waves.

Several monks and nuns of the Terapanth sect practice an *avadhana* known as *sapta sadhana*. This is a feat of grasping several objects simultaneously with the help of several organs. This is an example of *bahuvidhgrahi*. These are processes of training the mind.

Every human mind has immense power. It is practice which makes these powers operative. They often appear to be magical or supernatural when we watch it being practised by someone. But this is not so. These skills are a result of training and practice alone.

The third unit comprises *kshipgrahi* and *chiragrahi*. The former consists of grasping an object by intuitional flash. The mind is trained to develop photographic memory.

We are not aware of the abilities of our mind. It is very capable. We know very little about it. When we know little of its prowess, we are surprised. But if we knew all of it how amazed we would be! What all can happen, one does not know. When someone develops the mind a little, people start venerating him as god. It is good to become god, but it is even better to know that one can become godlike!

The other part of this unit is *chiragrahi*, which means a grasping power that works instantaneously but slowly. It takes a long time to master.

The fourth unit is composed of *anisritgrahi* and *nisritgrahi. Anisritgrahi* is the state of grasping the whole by seeing just a little; it is a combination of memory and intuition. A story illustrates this amazing skill very clearly.

A painter visited a king's court when from under the latticed door he caught sight of a beautiful toe. From that toe he imagined the entire person to whom the toe belonged. It happened to be that of the queen. He imagined with such accuracy that he even put the beauty spot in the right place, a place that was ordinarily covered. The king was enraged seeing that portrait. What access did the painter have to the queen that he knew of such details, wondered the king. The painter was sentenced to death, but a minister intervened and explained the special skill of the painter and so a life was saved.

Nisritgrahi is understanding an object that is fully visible. This is *avadhana* or merely the first stage while preparing the mind to meditate. If in this stage so much can be realized, one can only imagine the power that meditation can bring.

10
The Value of Thoughtlessness

As we are getting acquainted with the powers of the mind, can we make it competent enough to empty itself out? A competent mind is not our end goal. Our goal lies beyond the mind, in a state of thoughtlessness.

In order that we do not dissipate our energies in the phenomenal, we have to learn to tame the vanity of our sense organs that oppose the force of our innate knowledge of the world and the self. Then we reach that place where the fantasy woven by our senses falls off and we find our true self—the spirit it takes to uncover our true greatness. Samayika *is a practice of meditation as described by Mahavira, a method for gentle progression into a state of thoughtlessness.*

Our thinking is governed by a very small part of our consciousness. The transactions of human life do not seem to require more than a small amount of consciousness.

Sometimes we become spectators of our own consciousness, though not serious ones. There are a few who have the courage to dive into the depths of our consciousness just as divers do in search of precious stones. The depths of the consciousness are unfathomable. Consciousness is as infinite as the universe we live in. Imagination fails to comprehend it. We cannot imagine that there is a whole universe of consciousness behind and below the small part of it which governs our worldly life. Our minds are accustomed to act and think within certain limits. They cannot imagine a limitless and expansive consciousness.

Ground beneath the feet
There must be a path
Satisfaction in the heart
There must be a limit
Only Nothingness
Can be pathless and limitless.

The sense organs gather information for intellectual knowledge. But they have limitations. They can establish contact with gross things only. The mind works on the information supplied by the sense organs and the intellect organizes and arranges it. The knowledge which the mind and intellect construct is not pure knowledge—it is deeply influenced and coloured by our attachments and aversions, by our feelings of pleasure and pain. How much value should we place on this kind of knowledge? The knowledge which we have thus gathered is not as valuable as we think, for it has acquired the form it has because of the influence of our emotions. It is not pure knowledge. But we value that knowledge because we have not been able to go beyond the limitations of language. We value intellectual knowledge because we do not know that there is a state of mind in which thinking does not exist. We will have a strange and life-changing experience if we go beyond the pulls of worldly existence to where time moves very, very slowly.

It is only when we arrive at moments of complete absence of thinking that we are able to understand what we really are. Thinking is an all-pervading force and it is only when we eliminate it that we can realize the value of thoughtlessness.

Of course, the question remains as to how to emerge out of this state of constant thinking. We are swarmed by ideas, sounds, forms and bodies, and with continual interaction with them we are reduced to being conscious only of our body. The body, in fact, becomes a form in which the self is trapped. We cannot see anything beyond the body.

The vital force of the body is called prana. Prana is connected with the mind, *manasa*. *Manasa* is connected with buddhi, intellect. They all work concomitantly, one influencing the other and thus forming a vicious circle, from which it is difficult to break out of. We will not be able to appreciate the idea of pure consciousness until we are able to appreciate the idea of a thoughtless mind. The self can be known and realized only in those moments in which thinking has completely ceased. Thinking cannot lead to self-knowledge.

Many philosophers have worked on the subject of the self. Some have tried to prove its existence, and some disprove it. The self is not an object in the world of thought. That is why all attempts at discussing the nature of the self have failed. Only those who have transcended the level of thoughts, that is, those who have entered the thoughtless state, can speak with certainty about the nature of the self.

We are confronted with a process characterized by form and form alone. We cannot see the formless. The question therefore is, how can we see the formless and how can we understand the nature of pure consciousness? The relation between form and essence is the central question of epistemology. Man has devised the process of separating essences from their forms as in the case of fragrance from the flower. But how can the soul be separated from the body? How can we separate the finite from the infinite? The masters of yoga devised a method for doing so.

We can know the soul with the help of its reflection. When we stand in front of a mirror, we neither see our body nor the mirror, we see a reflection of our body. It is on this basis that we recognize our body. In the same way, there is a yogic practice known as sadhana of the *chhaya purusha*. The practitioner stands with his face towards the sun and looks at his shadow. Then he closes his eyes and again looks at the sun and then he looks at his shadow. This alternation continues till he can see his figure in the sky and the reflection of the sky in his shadow.

We can also see the soul in a thoughtless state when we can neither hear nor see. Preksha Dhyan is a process through which we can get rid of thoughts, sounds and forms and enter a state free of all thought. In those moments we would be able to catch a glimpse of the soul. Of course, one of the prime prerequisites to reach this state is to *just* see and *just* know. That is, the tendencies and inclinations of the mind, its attachments and aversions, have to be neutralized. Then we can catch a glimpse of the soul.

Perception and knowledge are means of knowledge of the self so long as they are not affected by external forces. As soon as we let the world influence us, we are pushed back into the world of thinking or the mind. It is rare to get to that state and rarer to stay there. We know most things only with the 'attachments' of likes and dislikes or such emotions. Take a flower, for example. We know it for its form, colour, beauty or fragrance. We cannot see or know the flower with the help of the mind, except in terms of the above-mentioned qualities or other similar ones. It is only when we raise ourselves from the limitations of language that we get a glimpse of the soul. Language binds us to the mind. Once we free ourselves from that we can progress into a state of thoughtlessness.

Words of thought that cross our mind pertain generally to memory, imagination or current happenings. Memory of the flower comes to the fore the moment a flower comes to our mind. There are place-related memories (*daishik smriti*) and time-related memories (*kalik smriti*). Imagination is an obstacle to concentration that could arise in the future. The mind is busy weaving dreams of what one could do. Imagination is not present reality. Needless to say, anything that happens occupies our mind and diverts it completely from concentrating. There is an old definition of concentration that goes like this:

> *Gyanantarasparshravarti gyansantati dhyanam*
>
> Concentration is that flow of consciousness which does not touch anything outside the consciousness. In it there is a perpetual contact with the 'self' and no contact with any 'other'.

Pindastha dhyana is the practice of concentrating the mind on the body. The object of *padastha dhyana* is the word.

Rupastha dhyana is concentration on form. *Rupatita dhyana* leads the practitioner above forms and dispositions. In this state, there is no object to be meditated upon. Meditation that implies thinking is simple meditation. A state of thoughtlessness is called samadhi.

How can we achieve the state of thoughtlessness? No straight answer to this is possible because it is an intellectual question. No living being which has a body, mind and intellect can, ordinarily, live in a state of thoughtlessness, just as no being which is subject to attachments, illusions, and so on, can be free of life's miseries. The state of thoughtlessness can be attained only through effort and practice.

It is a fact that too much thinking results in the loss of energy. As a matter of fact, all activity tires the body and drains its energy. Those who do intellectual work suffer from diseases of the stomach. Thinking is no doubt the function of the mind, but to go beyond limits is harmful.

Thoughtlessness is not a function of the body. It is the nature of the self and so involves no loss of energy. On the other hand, it produces additional energy in our body and mind.

The first thing we need to prepare ourselves to journey to this stage is patience. We should fix a target and begin with concentration of the mind. Once enough progress is achieved in getting rid of likes and dislikes, we should be able to develop the capacity to know. At this stage, we will be able to appreciate the state of thoughtlessness. Perception and thinking cannot go together. One who thinks does not know and one who knows does not think. Perception and knowledge belong to a different order. They are the natural attributes of a unified consciousness.

In Jaina philosophy the words *dhyana* and *samayika* are used. *Samayika* is a kind of meditation. Generally, when we speak of meditation, it means concentrating on an object or a symbolic image. The meditator remains distinct and separate from the object he is meditating upon. Besides the subject (the meditator) and the object (the article of meditation), there is a third element, which is the act of meditation. The practitioner must locate the object to meditate upon. In thoughtless meditation, the distinction between the meditator, the object of meditation and the act of meditating is absent. It is an indivisible state. The word *samayika* is derived from *samaya,* or the soul. *Samayika* means to be in the soul or the self. The one who has entered the soul leaves meditation behind. This is a state of complete thoughtlessness. He who has arrived at this state simply perceives and knows nothing but the soul. The process of thinking continues only until this state has been reached. It is better to use the term *samayika* instead of meditation. Mahavira used this term too.

A philosopher was delivering a long lecture on the soul. Suddenly, an impatient young scholar stood up and said, 'You are going on and on about something you have no proof of. I believe only that which I see. Show me the soul.'

The philosopher paused and said, 'I am tired after this long speech. I will show you the soul, but can you get me a glass of milk to re-energize myself?' The young man immediately got him a glass of milk.

Instead of drinking it, the philosopher kept peering into the glass. The young man peered too. What was wrong? 'Oh nothing,' said the philosopher, 'they say milk gives butter, clarified butter. I am searching for it.'

The young man laughed scornfully and thought this philosopher was obviously not well-read. 'To get clarified butter, you have to heat the milk, then set it with some curd. Once set it has to be churned to get butter.'

'That is the answer, my friend,' said the philosopher, 'To know the soul you have to put yourself through the heat of penance. Then settle your mind and concentrate. Thereafter, with some churning, the soul can be experienced.'

11
Inner Calm

There are two levels at which we can take our argument further: the practical level and the spiritual level. We are trying to look inwards and find our centre. This chapter is about the practical level.

At the practical level, we can all endorse the fact that with experience we are able to access many riches. But if we were to access inner calm, it would be the greatest blessing. There are many things to be gained in life, but perhaps nothing as valuable as inner calm. Whenever our inner calm is disturbed, everything in the world becomes meaningless and useless to us. A pure mind and a clear consciousness are the source of a beautiful life.

Is this just a rhetoric or a possibility? A great possibility.

Levels of consciousness

Just as we have different levels at which our mind operates, there are different levels of our consciousness too. We live at the level of the senses. There is another special level at which intuitive powers are awakened. At this level one gets a whiff of the past, of things far away and of unknown objects too. An even more evolved stage of the mind is the access to extrasensory perception, *ati indriya gyan*. At this stage external stimuli no longer matter. We are able to awaken the font of our knowledge that rests in our soul. We do not experience negative emotions at any of the evolved levels. It is only at the level of the senses that we have ideas of remiss, wrong, guilt and evil doings. If circumstances are favourable, we have positive thoughts; else, negative tendencies come to the fore.

Yogashastra has dealt with these stages very well. They say the mind is obstinate, rebellious and fickle. If we look at some aspects of our society, we may feel these are the tendencies that are at work now. When the mind is restless and rebellious these forces seem to be at work. If the mind is calmed down, and made to focus and meditate, these negative tendencies can be arrested. That is why we all look for inner calm; we all like to be at peace and happy.

If we look at these two states—restlessness and concentration of the mind—and assess a person's life based on these two, we will find that in the state of concentration, not just tendencies to commit wrongful acts but all other kinds of problems can be arrested. When the mind is restless, one encounters problems, unmanageable situations, disagreements and fights, and is led along a troubled route, ultimately getting entangled in them. It may even lead to us committing a crime. Restlessness is a big reason for crimes, huge or small. There are several levels of restlessness: slight, medium and extreme. The slightly restless mind does not cause itself much harm.

When restlessness is in the medium category, the doors to disputes and crime are opened and the restless mind either reacts impulsively or misinterprets easily, and so possibilities of indulging in undesirable activities increase. With extreme levels of restlessness, these possibilities turn into certainties.

How to attain inner calm?

Intoxicants, it is said, also give inner bliss. It is the restless mind that becomes easy prey to the use of intoxicants. We have always blamed any given situation for falling into the vicious cycle of habit-forming use of drugs and intoxicants. Rather, it is the restless mind that is to blame. This results in deformities of mind, body and action.

Let us reflect on circumstances. One of the important reasons for any sort of crime is the underdevelopment of the mind. When there is impairment or dullness in the mind, the tendency to indulge in deviant activities increases. Disagreements also depress the mind, turning it towards violence.

Under such conditions, intoxicants lend a sense of well-being and ecstasy. A research conducted on this found that different varieties of intoxicants are available in the world. It is not a new phenomenon. Man has used them to appease himself, if only to escape from disagreements. When one lives in a society, human interaction is bound to lead to some disagreements, fault-finding, condemnation, poverty and strife resulting from sorrow, unfulfilled expectations, depression and so on. These problems arise out of the tensions of the mind.

Man did not want to live a life of tension and so the solution he found was in intoxicants. They took him to a place where there were no problems, where worldly bliss could be experienced. It is not just the poor or the uneducated who took to them—the quick remedy spread across all social classes. It must be said that intoxicants do provide some relief, otherwise they would not be used so widely. But they leave behind horrible after-effects such as depression, dysfunction, laziness, distraction, a sense of being lost and so on.

If there are so many negative effects of intoxicants, why do so many still indulge in it? The reason is simple: people want to escape their problems and forget themselves, and go to a world where there are no responsibilities. Different drugs yield varied experiences. They all transport the addict to a magical world of continuous bliss.

In the Indian tradition, there have been two ways of looking at things: that which feels good in the beginning but does not yield good results, and that which is not so pleasant initially but is good in the long run. They are called *shreyas* and *preyas,* respectively. For an example, we may consider sugar and gooseberry. According to Ayurveda, sugar produces acidity and gooseberry purifies the system. In conditions of hyperacidity, gooseberry helps control it while sugar aggravates it. Sugar makes tasty sweets and desserts, while the gooseberry is quite sour to taste but good for the body in the long run. Intoxicants are those which are not known to produce even one good result for the body. But they give instant escape, not just from problems that exist but some that we may create for ourselves. Alcohol damages the liver. Tobacco damages the lungs and the heart. It can cause cancer. There is no intoxicant which does not harm the body. They belong to the category of *preyas*.

In today's rat race and materialism, it seems vacuous to talk of *shreyas*, that is, what is good for the human being or society. The priority is only on making money. Instead of values influencing vocation, corruption of all kinds has influenced it. No intelligent person would break the law. But, today, the mind has become so restless that even the law seems to hold no barrier, no threat. What does crime mean? Any act that transgresses the limits of social coexistence and creates problems is a crime, like theft, robbery and murder, among others. These showcase the working of an unhealthy mind, a mind with some deformity. Is there an escape? A healthy mind will not think of committing crimes.

Anuvrat

Anuvrat is the names of a movement launched by Acharya Tulsi in 1949. The philosophy behind this is that external control cannot control crime. The control must come from within. The practitioner of Anuvrat takes a few realistic pledges that are doable and abides by them.

Anuvrat asks how the problem of addiction could be tackled. This is an important question. How to put a stop to crime? The government uses law to enforce discipline. Every nation has massive budgets for law enforcement.

It is in this context that the Anuvrat movement was launched, but the experience was that de-addiction is difficult and required special yogic practices. So, a few Preksha

Dhyan workshops were also held simultaneously. Some simple exercises and practices requiring deep involvement were used.

The ear

Among the simple exercises, one is focussing on the ear. The ear is an important part of our body. It is the centre of alertness and righteous conduct. It is most often used as a spectacle-holder, little else. There is a practice to pull a child's ear as a manner of reprimand. The ear is an important psychic centre of the body and if we can focus our energies on the ear, we can give up addiction, almost automatically. Needless to say, the focus has to be intense and concentrated. Concentration upon the ear improves our mindfulness.

Mindfulness

Some intoxicants numb pain and even modern medicine uses them for anaesthesia and in small amounts in painkillers. We do not want to experience any pain, mental or physical, and will go to any extent to avoid it. So we numb our sensations. We do not feel anything. Sometimes we take a pill to dull our pain, and sometimes we resort to violence to numb our sensitivity. Even without consuming drugs we live, often, in a state of distraction, or illusion. It is in this state that we make mistakes.

Improving our alertness is called mindfulness. Meditation can be practised for an hour or two in a day, but one can be mindful every second of the day. To be mindful is to perform every action knowingly and deliberately. If this state is inculcated, then one will not need intoxicants. One will not be able to partake of intoxicants. One commits acts of self-destruction only when the consciousness is in delusion. Some medicines are also prescribed for de-addiction in homeopathy and Ayurveda, in addition to the practices of acupressure and acupuncture. But to be mindful is the easiest solution. This single practice can change our consciousness and our mind.

The message is loud and clear: as long as we look for external commands, instructions or stimuli to keep our life in order, we will be nurturing a restless mind which will, at the slightest provocation, succumb to pleasure-giving short-term remedies. Our character is built by developing our inner stability such that we do not require outer compulsions to live our life in order. Resolve. Meditate. Be your own police.

A meditational practice, *chaitanya kendra preksha* is described in Part 2, Chapter 2.

12

The Master of the Mind: Chitta

A thoughtless mind is the path to inner calm. Inner calm is the richest of riches, the coveted treasure. And yet, to an average person, it seems next to impossible to attain. Emotions torment us. Constant fears harass us. Sickness brings us down.

How to get to that elusive inner calm? What controls it? The chitta*—variously translated as the inner being, the subconscious, the part of consciousness that records desires, memories, feelings, emotions, attachments, aversion, thought patterns and impressions—is an energy field. The* chitta *controls the mind—and therefore the body.*

Mahavira, the twenty-fourth Tirthankara in the Jaina tradition, put himself through severe penance. Due to his extremely sturdy and healthy body, he was able to face many hardships, problems and calamities. A telling verse describes him thus:

Vapureva tavachaste, Bhagvana! Veetaragatam!
Na hi kotarasamsthegnati, tarurbhavati shadvarah

The verse extols Mahavira's strong body and asks, can a tree which has fire in its belly still be green? That is to say, when there are so many draining emotions in our system, such as anger, attachment, aversion in the body, how can the body remain healthy? It is because Mahavira has sublimated these emotions that his body is healthy. I will not be exaggerating when I say inner calm is the foremost requirement of health, and, to a large extent, vice versa.

The above verse further reiterates the idea we have encountered in the last chapter, that is, inner calm is an announcement of good health. The consciousness is radiant like the sun, and our inner self, one of its rays. The mind functions in association with the inner self. Our inner being is related to consciousness and the mind is related to matter. The consciousness of the mind that we experience is because of the inner being or *chitta*. The mind by itself is not animate. Then, what guides the *chitta*, the inner being? What guides the mind? The *chitta* is governed by the subtle body. The mind is governed by the *chitta*. So, the *chitta* creates the mind and our emotions. Vibrations from the subtle body reach the *chitta*, which is consciousness and which functions in association with the brain. These are called emotions.

Mahavira said, 'Man's *chitta* has many facets.' Some of them are as follows:

1. *Avarana chitta*
2. *Antaraya chitta*
3. *Mithyadarshana chitta*
4. *Moha chitta*

There are many more, but for the present discussion, these four are relevant. What is more, there are opposing *chittas* too.

1. *Anavarana chitta*
2. *Nirvighna chitta*
3. *Samyak-darshan chitta*
4. *Veetaraga chitta*

The starting point is *avarana chitta*, which means there is a veil of ignorance over the consciousness. A current that does not let the consciousness be uncovered emanates from the subtle body and envelops the consciousness. It does not bring about any disorder, just covers it, making direct access impossible.

Antaraya chitta is the current coming from within which creates obstacles. The individual cannot act or think as he wishes; there is always some deterrent blocking the way to it.

The third is *mithyatva chitta,* or the delusory outlook. The delusory outlook is primarily responsible for the absence of positive feelings. This does not permit the right view, or to assimilate reality. It changes one's outlook. The reality is something else, but experience or conviction tends to be different. It leads to *vimohatmaka khyati*, or what has been described in the philosophical world as the reversal of knowledge.

The fourth, *moha chitta*, does not allow one's character to develop properly. It does not allow the person to have a sense of self-restraint and impedes spiritual development. It takes one towards attachments and aversions, and the activities guided by them.

The other side

If we were guided by only these types of *chitta*, our life would be quite inferior. But the *chitta* has other aspects too. The positive sides. There is the *anavarana chitta*, which is the *chitta* that is not covered by a veil. A part of our consciousness is thus exposed. This exposure brings in knowledge. If the consciousness is fully covered, the object is inanimate. If the consciousness is partially exposed, we are talking of animate beings. The *anavarna chitta* does not let the consciousness be covered (by ignorance).

Nirvighna chitta is the *chitta* that leads to a state without obstacles. When you say about a person that there is nothing that can stop him, it means the *nirvighna chitta* is active. This person accomplishes much in this condition.

The third is the *samyak-darshan chitta*, which helps the individual develop the right perspective. This is the positive outlook.

The fourth is the *veetaraga chitta*. This helps the individual be more objective about life. It develops the character of a person.

It should be said that these *chittas* are present in all individuals, in some the first four take prominence and in others the second four. Everyone, for instance, has some good in them; the proportion varies with how active the *veetaraga chitta* is.

From the point of view of physical health, the *avarana chitta* is not connected with it, but is connected to knowledge. But the *antaraya chitta*, *mithyatva chitta* and, most of all, the *moha chitta* are closely connected with our health.

Let us divide the *chitta* into two parts—pure and impure. The purity of the *chitta* is related to the purity of the emotions and the mind. The mind inherently is not pure or impure—that is not the function of the mind. The function of the mind is to remember, imagine and think. It becomes pure or impure because of the flow of *chitta*. This flow gets transformed into *bhava* or emotion and this, in turn, influences the mind, making it pure or impure.

> The Mind
> A part of the body
> Since aeons
> Here lies an amusing tale.
> Caressed by consciousness
> The mind became immortal
> The poor body is, even now
> Seeking the way.

As a matter of fact, nothing about the mind is pure or impure. The wind is blowing. Is it hot or cold? If there is too much heat, the wind is hot, if there is a cold wave, the wind will be cold. Therefore, we cannot make a blanket statement; it is relative. That is how the mind is too. It has no independent existence.

The *chitta* has an independent existence. It is the function of the *chitta* to restrain the mind or let it free. If the *chitta* is pure and it has decided to restrain the mind, it will resort to *dhyana*. The *chitta* is the master of the mind.

We have encountered the concept of thoughtless meditation. The presence of consciousness is felt in that thoughtless state. Where there is constant experience of the consciousness and an awareness of the *chitta*, there is *dhyana*. In the absence of thought, there is no mind. But there is *dhyana*, because the awareness of one's existence or consciousness becomes sharp at that time.

Amana or the absence of the mind is an important word. The mind passes through various states, as we have seen, and the thoughtless mind is one of its states of being. The distinction that the *chitta* is enduring and that the mind is a creation should be clearly understood. What does this mean?

There is the mind if we create it. Where would the mind be if we did not create it? Mind, body and speech are three aspects of our life. Among them, mind and speech are the same. The body exists if there is life in it. But we create mind and speech and rest them when we want. That is why the mind is not situated anywhere. This is not the case with the *chitta*. It cannot be created. Just as the body is always with us, so is the *chitta*. The *chitta* will always be with us and continue to function, whether we are asleep or awake. That is why the sages raised the following questions in the *Nyayashastras*: who had a sound sleep? The mind was inactive. Who experienced the quality of sleep? The *chitta* did.

The *chitta* is a ray of consciousness. It is necessary to clarify that the *chitta* and the mind are separate. The first creation of the *chitta* is *bhava*. The mind is not the first creation of the *chitta*. The *chitta* creates *bhava* from within. All our emotions are creations of the *chitta*. That is why the *chitta* is of several types. On the basis of an emotion, one can categorize the *chitta* as one of anger, vanity, greed, hatred, quarrelsome and so on. These *bhavas* pass into the mind. The mind does not create them. The *chitta* creates them and sends them to the mind. The *bhava*, once it comes into the mind, is called *manobhava*.

When the concept of the mind was examined in Agama literature, the Sankhya philosophy and the Rig Veda, it was concluded that its function was to reflect and think. Today, in the world of artificial intelligence, they say even computers will be able to reflect. What happens to consciousness? The computer functions mechanically. The mind too is a machine, a tool of the *chitta*. Whatever a computer thinks will have no impact on the existence of the soul because thinking is not a basic function of the soul or the *chitta*, it is only a side activity. The basic function of the *chitta* is to experience, wish and feel. The mind has no wish of its own, although litterateurs and saints have said the cravings of the mind know no limits. The mind has no cravings. How can the mind, which is created with the body, have endless craving?

Desire is said to be a basic human character. It is present even in those beings which do not have a developed mind. That is, the *chitta* has been considered as the basic characteristic of a living being, not the mind. All living beings have desire. What gives rise to desire? The *chitta* does.

Chitta, mind and bhava

Let us understand the relation between *chitta*, mind and *bhava*. From the point of view of meditation, *chitta*, mind and *bhava* form a complete chain, linking the subtle and the gross world. From a health point of view, if mind, *bhava* and *chitta* are impure, they would create problems. If these three are pure, good health will prevail. Psychosomatic illnesses are a result of an impure *chitta*. Mahavira believed a pure *chitta* brings good health with pure *bhava* and mind.

The discussion of the relation between the mind and the *chitta* is crucial to understand the health of a being. It is not a philosophical discussion. The person who wishes to be healthy should have good nutrition. Similarly, he should also have a clean and pure *chitta*. Bad thoughts and ill feelings sully the *chitta*. They send unhappy emotions to the mind which affects the body. We know that the healthiest of persons fall prey to many diseases which are said to be stress-related or born of depression and other psychological ailments. These arise in the *chitta*. So, for good health, we must ensure that we have a pure and clean *chitta*.

A young man approached a guru and said, 'Sire, I want to learn the secret of truth from you.'

'I will teach you,' said the guru. 'Come, live with me.'

The young man moved in with the guru. The guru told him to collect firewood, light the fire, buy provisions and cook. Then he had to clean up. The disciple followed his instructions. Day after day the routine was the same. Year after year the routine was the same.

After twelve long years of the same routine, the guru called his disciple one day and said he could leave.

'But, sire, you have not taught me anything.'

'You have worked these twelve years with unswerving rectitude. Continue to develop this pure consciousness and you will reap rich rewards. That is sadhana or penance.'

The disciple immediately felt an awakening inside. He had become a wise sage.

13

Keep the Body Healthy

Health is a must to achieve anything. And when we talk of success in life, good health is also as much a measure of success as other material pointers are. At one level, we understand that the chitta *keeps us healthy. At another level we need to pay attention to our physical body in terms of illnesses, nourishment, exercise and maintaining good health. It is not limited to eating a balanced diet, but it involves a deeper understanding not just of how different foods impact us differently but also a shift from curative medicine to preventive action.*

Who does not want to be healthy? That has been man's foremost desire. Medicine addresses this desire in two ways: one, by trying to maintain good health and two, by treating ill health. It will not be wrong to say that preventive or wellness medicine has not developed as much as curative medicine.

Modern medicine focuses on cures. Ayurveda and naturopathy address the need for health to prevent diseases and the need for a cure that arises.

The first question is, who can be considered healthy? Ayurveda says the one whose soul and senses are happy is healthy. The hidden indicators are balanced humours and balanced *agni* or digestive fires (*samadoshosamaagnishch*). But when you see a person is happy from within and the senses are in gentle operation, you say he is healthy (*prasannatmoindriyaman*).

Physiological perspective

From a physiological point of view, one may say that if the digestive system works well, the food eaten is assimilated and the excretory system performs its function of throwing out the waste, the person is healthy. If we go one step further, we would say that the one whose nervous and endocrine systems work well is healthy. Going further still, in ancient texts, that person is labelled healthy whose bone structure is well formed for it is on that skeleton that the body rests. In Jaina texts, even learning and knowledge accumulation are described on the basis of the strength and arrangements of a person's bones: a person's knowledge is proportionate to the quality of his bone structure. His meditative knowledge and strength of meditation are assessed based on the strength of his bones. The bone marrow contains a large part of inherited traits and knowledge. This perspective, it should be remembered, is largely based on karmic legacies. It is not a reflection of the nourishment one has got in the present birth.

Our physical health is critically dependent on the spinal cord (*sushumna*). The spine has thirty-three vertebrae. The more flexible they are, the better the health of the person. That is why yoga is advocated for good health. It keeps the body flexible. Examination of the spinal cord alone can reveal the health of a person. If the spinal cord is bent and stiff, it is a sign of deteriorating health.

The two lines below in Sanskrit describe health.

Suasthi asti yasya sa swasthaha: The one whose bone structure is good is healthy.

Swasmin tisttathi iti swastha: The one who lives within himself is healthy.

The second one is an intellectual proposition. Our bone marrow and grey matter store information of many births. So, the quality of the bone marrow is closely linked with and determines the quality of a person's health. The bone marrow, as has been mentioned in the previous paragraph, contains a large part of inherited traits and genetic knowledge, and it is in this context that this statement is to be understood.

These being the many ways of looking at defining health, we may move on to discuss what keeps good health. Nutrition is, of course, foremost. We are all familiar with the term and the need for a balanced diet: it should have proteins, fats, carbohydrates, vitamins and minerals in the right measure. Yet, we seek betterment of our health and the food we eat.

Right quantity of food

In the principles of Preksha Dhyan, attention has been paid to the kind of food one must consume for good health. An important point, in addition to a balanced diet, is to take the right quantity of food, just enough to meet our body's requirements. Even if the food is tasty, of very good quality and very well balanced, it will be detrimental if taken in larger quantities. There are many ways in which one could judge the benefits of the foods consumed.

Do not eat those items which are inimical to each other.

Are we eating two things which do not get on well with each other? For example, drinking a cold glass of milk after a heavy meal, or combining musk melon and milk will cause indigestion and production of toxins in the body. These edibles do not gel well and should not be eaten together.

Are we eating age-appropriately?

According to Ayurveda, health is defined by the balance of *doshas*: *vatha* (wind), *pitta* (bile) and *kapha* (phlegm). Up to the age of forty, *kapha* dominates. For the next thirty years, *pitta* dominates, and finally *vatha*. Accordingly, the person should not eat much of the food that contains the humour that is dominant; for example, after the age of seventy a person should not eat food that creates *vatha*, like potatoes.

Are we eating time-appropriately?

According to Ayurveda, the humours of the body vary with the time of the day. The first part of the day is dominated by *kapha*, the second by *pitta* and third part by *vatha*. Therefore, foods like musk melon or guava should not be eaten in the evening. One should know which food should be eaten at which time of the day. Food does not digest well after sunset and so it is advised to eat before sunset.

Are we taking *svarshastra* into consideration?

The breath is called *svar*. At any point of time, one nostril is more active than the other. Accordingly, food should be eaten when the *svar* of the right nostril (sun) is operating and water consumed when the *svar* of the left nostril (moon) is operating. Good health can get disturbed if done otherwise. The right nostril is associated with our body's heating energy and so referred to as the sun nostril while the left is with our body's cooling energy and so called the moon nostril.

Food should be justly earned

Our health is related not only to material substances but also to our attitudes and mental states. Food earned through evil means—that is, guile, deceit, fraud and craftiness—affect the body negatively. Food should be eaten only when one is hungry. I have always maintained that spirituality or moral rectitude comes only after the basic needs are met. Paucity mars human character. A hungry and poor man may steal, may try to get food through evil means, but that is for his survival and so we cannot advise him.

Avoid reaction

One of the principles of good health is to avoid reaction. When we have extreme anxiety or anger, it affects our digestive system. We have dealt with the need to control reaction earlier. We arrived at the conclusion that reaction is violence. Now we can see it is violence not just to another but also to our own body.

Health and friendship

Practice amity. They reduce toxins in the body and help to keep better health. The emotion of hatred is dangerous to the one who nurtures it—it is a poison of the mind. The *Sthanang Sutra*, a Jaina text, enumerates seven ways in which a person dies without dying physically.

Thought activity

While eating, one should concentrate just on that activity. One should not think other thoughts. Charaka, one of the main Ayurvedic doctors of ancient India, said: *Prasanna mana bhunjita*, or eat with a happy mind.

Restrain from speaking

The day should be calculated in terms of the periods of silences we can observe. One of the three ways of dissipating our energies is through excessive talking. The other two are excessive thinking and excessive activity. Thus, restraint in speaking is an important sign of good health.

Sleep

Ayurveda speaks of three secondary supports of health. Breath or vital energy is the main support which helps us preserve health. It has three secondary supports: food, sleep and *brahmacharya* (conduct of rectitude). We have discussed food above. Sleep is extremely important. Without it, health is inconceivable. Even a day's loss of sleep disturbs your daily rhythm. In modern times, sleeplessness has become a major problem. Even as tension is a universal disease, sleeplessness is acquiring the same proportions.

Moral rectitude

The third secondary support is *brahmacharya*. In literal translation, it means practising moral rectitude. It has been translated loosely as celibacy in many texts. It is actually a word with far greater connotations. Right conduct means restraint of all sense organs.

We have many hospitals coming up every day and yet they are not enough. There is a proliferation of new diseases: HIV-AIDS, plague and bird flu, among others. These are the result of man's unchecked self-gratification. As we have seen earlier, even the best things for us can turn poisonous if indulged in beyond limits. It is necessary to understand the role of all activities and not overdo them.

Finally, we have faith in curative health and less in preventive health. That is where the core of the problem lies. How much time do we spend in maintaining good health? Only when we fall ill do we run for medical help.

Preksha Dhyan

In Preksha Dhyan, emphasis is laid on developing the consciousness to keep good health. The first step is to make people aware of their health. The second step is to educate them about their health. These two steps alone will take one a long way.

Ayurveda classifies illnesses into four categories. Two of them are a result of one's karma. They are healed by purifying the soul. (This is explained in the context of the religious beliefs of the Jainas in subsequent chapters.)

The other two are seasonal, like cold or flu, which can be prevented, and we can also save ourselves from other, more complicated problems if we take care of our diet.

Asana

I consider asanas or postures an important part of Preksha Dhyan. If we do not practice asanas along with meditation, the digestive system is weakened. Meditation requires quite a bit of energy and if we do not support it with pranayama and asanas, our digestive system will go for a toss. So, we practice those asanas that keep us in balance.

There are two types of pranayama, one meant for the body and the other for meditation. We must practice both as per need.

In Takshila University, there lived a teacher of medicine called Acharya Atreya. He sent his disciple, Kumar Jivaka, to the woods, saying, 'Go to the forest in the city's outskirts and get me those plants that cannot be used as medicine.' The disciple left to carry out his teacher's orders. He searched and he searched. Finally, he was exhausted. He came back empty-handed and presented himself to the acharya. The acharya asked, 'Child! Have you not followed my orders?'

The disciple answered, 'Sir, from morning till nightfall, I have roamed the forest. I have searched every nook and corner of it. But I could not find even one plant that did not have medicinal value.'

The teacher was pleased, 'You have learnt the science of healing. Your education is complete.'

Just as there is no herb that does not have any value, there are no asanas which do not bring any benefit. We just have to understand them and practice them correctly. If we take care of our body based on all of the above-stated ideas, we may keep good health for most of our life.

14

Keep the Mind Healthy

The mind is also capable of falling ill. The mind has been classified as having different traits. The stable one is, of course, the healthiest. The healthy mind has high forbearance. Forbearance requires courage. A healthy mind is a courageous one. It assists the intellect in wise decision-making and building a good memory. All these are prerequisites for greatness of any kind.

Some practices which help the development of these traits have been identified.

The body is gross and visible. The mind is subtle. It cannot be seen and is visible only through its actions. The body, the senses and the mind come together in our lives. The mind manages the body's senses. The information collected by the senses is organized by the mind. Without it, each of the sense organs would operate independently, if they did at all, and there would be no coordination between them, and we would be unable to make any progress in life. The mind is different from the brain. It is true without the brain, none of the sense organs would function, but without the linkages with the mind, the sense organs still do work.

The mind promotes and collates information. Imagination, memory, thoughts, arguments—they all come to the mind. The mind is useful to us but that which is useful can also be bothersome at times. The great physician Charaka had written that the mind and body are shelters for illnesses. Both can fall ill. A healthy mind and body are of great benefit to us. An unhealthy mind can cause great harm to itself and others.

Willpower and sorrow

If everyone could develop willpower, there would be fewer problems in the world. It is said that the ignorant finds the world full of sorrow whereas the knowledgeable finds it full of bliss. When it was asked if the world is full of darkness or light, the answer given by Mahavira was that to the blind man, the world is a dark place. After all, only the eyes can see light. Similarly, the knowledgeable knows bliss, the ignorant, who can also be called weak or with no willpower, finds the world to be full of sorrow. The one who has a strong will has fewer problems whereas the one with a weak will is immersed in sorrow.

Mahavira said there are four types of mental traits:

1. *Hrim sattva*
2. *Hrim manaha sattva*
3. *Chal sattva*
4. *Sthir sattva*

The *hrim sattva* person has strong willpower. He is so shy and self-disciplined that he will not give voice to any of his problems. Nor will he let it show in his fear or physical demeanour. No event affects him mentally.

The one with *hrim manaha sattva* has a strong willpower and does not let anything affect his mind, but his body succumbs to it and his physical health may suffer.

The *chal sattva* person is one who has a restless mind. He cannot concentrate on anything, always flitting from one thought to another.

The one with *sthir sattva* is stable. Nothing affects his mind.

A robbery once took place in a rich man's house, and a bit of money was stolen. The rich man was a *sthir sattva* person and so when people came to express their sympathy, he told them it was no big deal.

'So much wealth has been stolen and you think it is not a big deal?'

'Yes,' replied the man, 'Wealth comes and goes. I only earned that. I will earn more.'

His wife had a *chal sattva*. She was devastated and started crying. Unable to calm her, the husband asked a monk who was visiting them to assuage her fears. 'I am the one to earn, why is she crying?' he asked.

The monk asked the wife what was bothering her.

'Sir, a lot of money has been stolen.'

'Do you have a well in your house?'

'Yes, sir, we do.'

'Does it have water?'

'Yes, sir, it does.'

'Has all the wealth and treasures you have been stolen?'

'No sir, quite a bit remains.'

'How are your relatives, your servants etc., behaving?'

'As usual, very well, sir. No change.'

'Then why are you upset? Sages have said that there are three gems in the world: water, grain and good words. You have a well with water in your house. Your granary is full. And your family members are well spoken. Then why are you sad? He is stupid who thinks of a stone as a gem and cries over it.'

The wife was truly convinced that the true gems, water, grain and good words, she had in plenty and so became calm and stable.

The *chal sattva* person would like to flow with the tide, even if it is in the wrong direction, while the *sthir sattva* person will decide based on what is good for the future and not be influenced by the momentary mood.

Once a monk was resting close to a stream. He sent his disciple to fetch drinking water from the clear stream. As the disciple was about to fill up a jug, a bullock cart crossed the stream, muddying the water. The disciple returned to the teacher and told him the water was not potable. The teacher bade him to sit. After ten minutes, he again sent him to the stream for water. This time the water was clean and he filled the jug with it.

'The water is very clear. You said it was muddy?' asked the teacher.

'A bullock cart had crossed the stream and muddied the water,' replied the disciple.

'My child, a decision should not be taken on the basis of the circumstances, but on the true nature of anything. The stream is not impure, its water is pure. At that moment it appeared muddy, and on that basis, you declared it unfit for drinking.'

The one with a *chal sattva* takes decisions on the basis of the prevailing circumstances. Today, social sciences have become like that—studying only the circumstances and taking decisions based on them. We have forgotten the true nature of the human being. As a result, we commit mistakes and live in illusions. Circumstances have their short-lived value, but they do not last. If we can make decisions looking at basic human nature, then many decisions will be made correctly.

The Gita, Sankhya philosophy and Charaka have tried to analyse and understand the mind based on the three qualities of *sattva*, *rajas* and *tamas*. Broadly speaking, one may say *sattva* qualities are those that maintain harmony in and around a person. That implies purity, gentleness, righteousness and a forgiving nature. *Rajas* represents aggression, energy, passion and action. This person is generally a go-getter. *Tamas* is the quality of lethargy. So, a *tamasic* person is slow, associated with all that is not progressive.

Willpower and forbearance are great strengths. Let us understand that there is a close relationship between the mind, willpower and forbearance. The intellect and the mind have different jobs. The mind's job is to build forbearance. The intellect has no capacity to forbear. The capacity to tolerate lies with the mind. A person with a healthy mind will be able to withstand any situation. The health of the mind is thus judged by *sahishnutha* or forbearance.

On the basis of *rajas*, *tamas* and *sattva*, the conclusion that Susruta, another great ancient Indian physician, came to was the one with dominant *sattva* has the highest forbearance and the one with *tamas* has the least. The one with *rajas* does not have the ability to forbear, but with a little support from a wise counsel it may be able to. The one with *tamas* cannot have forbearance even with good counsel.

The one with *sattva* can put up with anything. Whatever situation a person faces, he or she can find an argument which makes the situation tolerable.

Dhriti, or endurance

This is the second anvil on which mental health can be judged. How much courage do you have? That person is courageous who does not buckle under pressure. When faced with adversity he who still holds his own is the courageous one. The Sumeru mountain is a good example. In the *Bhaktamar Stotra*, Rishabh, the first Tirthankara, is likened to Sumeru—when winds strong enough to uproot mountains raged, it stood its ground.

If one has endurance, all problems are as good as solved, all sorrows as good as overcome.

Buddhi, or intellect

The third touchstone of mental health is intellect. Its job is to decide, to be wise, and willpower assists it. If a person's mental health is good, he makes the right decisions and uses his intellect well. If his mental health is unstable, then his power of decision-making is poor.

Smriti, or memory

The third touchstone of mental health is memory. To have good memory is a sign of good mental health. When there is any distortion, any depression, the memory weakens. To not lose one's memory is a sign of good mental health.

Control your mind

Physical ailments do not harass man as much as mental health ailments do. I have seen many patients with problems of the mind come to attend the Preksha Dhyan training camps. Their world seems to be one of sorrow. Even though they have every joy in the world, they are miserable because their mind falters. We look after our body better than our mind. A wise man would spend twenty per cent of his time on his body and fifty per cent on his mind. After all, the mind runs the body—if the mind is not healthy how can the body be?

A sutra: Preksha Dhyan and mental health

To keep the mind strong, it is important to keep it empty. If we work the mind overtime—thinking continually, recollecting, imagining and so on—it will get tired and fall ill. A beautiful sutra to keep a healthy mind is to give it rest, to empty it out. Thinking is a good activity but not continually. Imagining is good but not continually. Control all of them, empty the mind and keep it healthy.

One method is to practice *swaspreksha*. The one who practises breathing exercises can empty his mind. To concentrate is to give the mind the best tonic. This gives it far more energy than anything else. Practise drawing long breaths for ten minutes two or three times a day. You will find your mind relaxing.

The thoughtless state

We have already discussed how a thoughtless state can benefit the mind. It can improve willpower and even bring longevity.

Some useful practices

Mahavira gave some practices that can help influence the mind. Patanjali yoga too has some suggestions to that end. These practices are based on the principle that sound and light waves influence and impact the mind. Certain sounds and certain colours have greater impact. Detailed discussions on which colour emits what kinds of waves and how it influences the mind are found in both yogic texts and Jaina texts.

Leshya dhyana is a meditation with colours. This meditation is based on the principle that all colours emit waves and impact the mind. To understand its fundamental principle, we have to go back to some fundamental principles of Jaina thought. Consider how we commonly feel about the self. We associate it with 'I' and 'mine'. I did this, I think like this, I want to achieve this. Equally we say this house is mine, this achievement is mine and so on. These feelings create their allies and form their own strategies in our minds. Attachment and hatred are born of them. When we are infatuated by someone, attachment develops, and the feeling of hatred develops for the one we dislike. Attachment and hatred have their own world and they are the creators of that world. The products of their creation is termed *kashaya* or passions. Anger, pride, delusion and greed are the creations of attachment and aversion, as also are fear, loathing, lust and sorrow. All are born of attachment and hatred.

Kashaya literally means to paint in one's own colours. The hues of anger or greed may imbue one's consciousness and hence render it impure. A coloured glass prevents us from seeing the true colour, and makes the entire world appear to have the colour of that glass. Similarly, the *kashaya* lends colour to our consciousness. The existence of *kashaya* causes instability in the activity of the mind, speech and body. *Leshya* meditation is the use of colours to counter the colours of the consciousness and thereby cleanse it, purify it.

This particular practice involves the colours green and white. These colours influence the mind in such a way that it turns inwards. In other words, they make one introspective. If one could concentrate on the colour green on the *darshan kendra*, the mind would find peace. To meditate on white on the *jyoti kendra* benefits the mind enormously. (This will be clear after the chapter on Preksha Dhyan.)

Mahaprana dhvani is beneficial for the mind and strengthens it. It is a humming sound, like that of a bee. If practised for ten minutes in a day, it has the power to energize the mind.

Sarvendriya sayam mudra: Our senses weaken our mind. It takes the mind towards temptations and makes it restless. If we cut our connection with the outside world by blocking our senses, then automatically our mind will get the rest it needs. This practice involves closing the ears with the thumbs, the eyes with the first two fingers and the nose with the third finger and the mouth with the fourth. This practice cuts off the outside world and even five minutes of doing this gives a relaxation equivalent to three hours of sleep. It is the practice of going from duality to singularity, from a crowd to solitude.

Experience a state beyond grief

All these practices enumerated above are very good for mental health. Through them we can restructure and develop our mind. We can overcome anguishing circumstances that weigh us down today, bring us ill health or weaken us. Materialism and mental ill health seem to have an inverse relationship. We find the cases of mental illnesses increasing day by day. It is important to keep our mind healthy and find solutions that keep our mind in a fit state, in addition to our body. Then problems and sorrows will no longer belong to our world, we would have passed them by into a brand-new, healthy and positive world.

15
Keep the Emotions Healthy

Not being swayed by emotions helps with decision-making. The best decisions come from a calm mind. How to send such emotions to the mind?

There are two separate flows of emotions in our body: one, which promotes negative emotions like arrogance, anger and jealousy; and two, which promotes humility, gentleness and peace of mind. To choose the latter to be dominant will help change the world we live in, not only for ourselves but for others too. In this case, emulating someone you think is perfect can help.

The body and mind express themselves in the outside world. Emotional health is a matter of the inner world. We keep having experiences within us which we are aware of most of the time, but perhaps are rarely aware of their underlying cause. In Preksha Dhyan, we ask to see the soul through the soul. The meaning is to travel within and see what is taking place.

We overburden our mind. Like flogging a dead horse, we are relentless. The question is, who bears the burden? If we find an answer to this question, we will find the inner world is vast and plagued by emotional turmoil.

We have certain beliefs and notions—so-and-so is nice and such-and-such is not nice, this person wishes me well and that one does not—and we get set in our ways. Who is this who is feeling all this and why? This is not the job of the mind. The mind just thinks, imagines and recollects. Who believes this to be true? We have not lavished as much attention on our emotions as we have on our mind. The reason for what we consider to be true are our emotions, and this is where much of our life is being enacted.

The main source of our feelings, however, is the soul. The consciousness of the soul finds expression. Its first cover is the karmic body.* Vibrations come from there. The other body is the *tejas* body which is what makes our aura radiant. The vibrations from the karmic body take form in the *tejas* body, lending it colour called *leshya* and translating feelings into emotions. These emotions go to our hypothalamus and influence our mind. The inanimate mind is thus impacted by emotions. This is the difference between the mind and the psyche.

Man gets angry, and egoistic, he cheats and deceives, feels greed, fear, hatred and lust—these emotions are not visible outside, they remain within and find expression through the mind.

---

* There are five types of bodies. The subtlest one is the karmic body, made up of our deeds. The next subtle body is the *tejas* body, which is a luminous, electric body. The *audarik sharir* or the gross body, the subtle transformational body and the translocational body are the other three.

Life is a constant struggle, not only with the circumstances that prevail outside but also within us rages a constant struggle. According to the theory of karma, there are two words to describe this: *kshayopashamik bhava* and *audyogik bhava*. *Kshayopashamik* means partial purity, brought on by the qualities of faith and good conduct. We have encountered the word *kashaya* earlier. *Kshayopashamik* means cleansing of the consciousness of emotions through right conduct. The *audyogik bhava* increases the feelings of arrogance, trickery and jealousy in a person. There is a continuous tussle between these two traits. *Kshayopashamik bhava* supports the sublimation of passions and the development of humility, gentleness and other sattvic qualities. The *audyogik bhava* supports anger, arrogance and other negative emotions. So, the two constantly clash.

It is necessary to work on one's emotions so that we weaken the negative thoughts and strengthen the goodness in us. In other words, we have to develop and harness the *kshayopashamik bhava* so that we can live in peace and amity. Nowadays it is widely accepted that war begins in the mind before it reaches the battlefield. Mahavira enumerated ten types of weapons that are used for war. The tenth weapon is emotion. Violence and war are born first in the emotional world. It is there that they all begin. In the outer world, we see their expression.

The inner world cannot be seen or described adequately in words. The external world can be described in words.

In Sankhya philosophy, the earth is called *gandhavati*. *Gandh* means perfume or aroma. How does the earth get its scent? The phenomenon of petrichor is not expressed till rain falls on dry soil and a beautiful aroma is born. Similarly, emotions are hidden in our inner world and all our problems occur there before they come out into the outer world. Just like a foetus is alive and active in the womb, but we record its life only after it is born in the outer world. Now, science has shown us the developments that take place inside the womb. So, too, our emotions work inside our body. Knowing alone is not enough, in this case. We must make the effort to change our emotional nature to a conducive one.

Why? The greatest concern is maintaining peace in the world. Internal peace for the individual, societal peace for a community and international peace for coexistence. This is possible only when each one of us is peaceful at heart. And this is possible only when our emotions are pure.

The first step in this direction is to choose an ideal. An ideal is different from a teacher. A teacher shows you the direction, tells you the dos and don'ts. An ideal says nothing—just remains a silent beckoning goal. The ideal cannot be another living human being because a living human being will give opinions and instructions when you go to him with a problem. This will further create confusion in the mind. However, if the living being is a realized soul then he or she can be the ideal. The ideal is beyond the mind and the world of emotion. The sutra of yoga is to establish harmony with the ideal. Install the ideal in the *shakti kendra* and meditate upon it there. Whenever any emotional problem arises, meditating can help in dealing with it considerably. Once we establish the supreme in our hearts, we establish the highest expression of compassion, joy or peace within us. Remember, Jainism does not believe in a Creator or God. So, when I say supreme, I do not necessarily mean God. If you worship a god, by all means, install Him or

Her in your heart. Else, it could be an ideal which has attained realization. Then we can keep borrowing it as the source to flow within us. We are constantly being bombarded by our emotions—happy, upset, tired, energetic—there is a constant emotional churning within us.

A man threw a lavish feast. He invited all the bigwigs of the town. He served them himself. In Rajasthan, serving lentil chips called papad at the end of the meal is a tradition. By the time he reached the last person, the papad had broken into bits. The man who was to be served had a big ego. His inner being rose up in turmoil. He thought, everyone was given a full unbroken papad, but only I got a broken one. He resolved to take revenge.

A few days later, he threw a lavish party at his home and invited the same group of people who had been at the earlier party. He served everyone full papads and to the man who had served him, he broke it into pieces before serving him. It did not affect that man as he had humility. He felt that a papad could be eaten only by breaking it, so what if it was broken already? The man who had planned this revenge was disappointed with his reaction. Unable to bear it, he finally asked, 'How did you like your papad?'

'Oh, it was great,' the man replied.

'Ah! You did not realize you got bits of papad, not a papad.'

'Ha! No problem, it saved me the job of breaking them.'

'Do you realize this happened because you served me broken papad at your house?'

'Oh! Did that make you throw the party? If only you had told me then, I would have gone in and got you a full one.'

Our world of emotions is a strange place. It will indeed be gratifying to see a pure inner self, unsullied by the mesh of emotions. But this is not easy. It requires hard work and penance. Those who put in the effort not just learn for themselves but also benefit the world. But, again, it is not easy.

To change the flow of emotions and ensure uninterrupted happiness, unstinted joy and a peaceful mindset, it is important to fix the ideal. To establish the objective and blissful ideal on the *shakti kendra*, thus, stop the flow of *audyogik* emotions and become the source of *kshayopashamik*.

The area between the eyebrows and around them is very important. Two glands, the pituitary and the pineal, work there. The pineal gland is where our intuitive power rises.

A blind man once went to Lord Jesus. The Lord was compassionate and restored his sight. One day, as the Lord was walking, he saw a young man running after a courtesan. The Lord summoned him and asked, 'Did I not restore your eyesight? Only for you to chase skirt?'

Replied the youth, 'Sir, you gave me eyesight, but not insight—so I indulge in what I should not.'

The *shakti kendra* is an important psychic centre of our body. If we meditate on it, our flow of emotions will be purified. Meditate on the colour white, with the ideal established there, and it will help to alter the flow of emotions. One simply has to make the effort.

Emotions and colours

The world is full of colour. We eat fruits that are so vibrant. In fact, all food has its own colour. At a certain frequency of vibrations, colours become visible to us. There is a principle of *leshya* in Jaina texts which is based on an understanding of colours and their impact on the human body, particularly, on emotions.

An interesting conversation took place between Mahavira and his disciple Gautama:

'O Lord! A person commits violence, how many colours does violence have? How many smells? How many tastes? How many touches?'

The foremost question was on colour and Mahavira replied, 'Five colours.'

The question and answer might seem strange. But not when it is explained in terms of colours. It is believed that when a colour has a negative effect on a person, it causes him or her to commit violence.

The *leshya* has colour particles which influence our *bhava-dhara* or emotions. One of the meanings of *leshya* is colour. The other is emotions. With the dominance of a certain colour, a person would feel a certain way. Colour and emotions have a close, and pervasive, influence on each other. For example, with a surfeit of red, the person feels aggression. Blue, on the contrary, is calming.

Our body is surrounded by colours. Those emanating from the body are called *abhamandal*. The halo around a person's head is called the *bhamandal*. The purer the *abhamandal*, the healthier that person is, physically, mentally and emotionally. To read the *abhamandal* requires expertise, but it is believed that it can predict a disease up to six months in advance.

It is believed that when a person becomes too violent there is an accumulation of black colour, or darkness, in the person's heart and mind. This is called *krishna* or black. By changing the *leshya* one can impact the emotional traits too. If the *abhamandal* has lot of blue, it is indicative of a jealous type. However, if the *abhamandal* is radiant it means the emotions are positive and the person is gentle and polite. Detailed descriptions of the *leshya* and the emotional state have been given in the Jaina text called the *Uttaradhyayana Sutra*. Colour therapy, along with sound and smell therapies, is used for influencing emotions with the belief that if emotions are balanced, health can be restored.

16

Greatness and Fame

We have learnt to organize our existence: by trying to accept our interdependence with all beings, living and non-living.

We have learnt to organize our intellect: by trying to accept that opposites coexist (anekanta) and thus allowing for differences.

We have learnt to organize our mind: by trying to still it with concentration and meditation.

We have learnt to organize our emotions: by trying to influence the chitta *or the psyche, also through meditation.*

But look around you. So much clutter! Clutter, though comprising of inanimate objects, can make you less efficient than you actually are.

Go to the source of the clutter. Learn to differentiate between need and want, between fame and greatness.

The difference between fame and greatness is that which separates from the humane and the inhumane.

As we have seen, the emphasis in Jainism and in Mahavira's teachings has been on relativity. Everything is relative. Many branches of study are interlinked. For example, even though economics deals with the optimum use of limited resources, it cannot be examined in silo. If it does, as we sometimes think it does, the study is never accurate, and we find many problems on our plate.

The British economist John Maynard Keynes said that the primary aim of economics is to economically empower the poorest. The aim is laudable and not very different from that of communism or capitalism. The means and method may be different. One meaning of development is that every person should be able to access basic necessities and have a good living standard. Economic development also has a similar aim: increase in the per capita income.

No one desires poverty. It has been said that the one who is poor is weak—*adhanam nirbalam*. Poverty has always been considered a curse and from no perspective has it been viewed as favourable.

A learned man was on his way to meet Raja Bhoj, a wise king. The man was very poor. All he could get for the king, by way of gift, were two small pieces of sugarcane. As he had to walk a long way, he sat down to rest under a tree in a forest. Soon he fell asleep. At that time, another passer-by noticed him sleeping and the two sugarcane pieces sticking out of his bag. The hungry man found two wooden pieces of similar length and, pulling out the sugarcane, placed the sticks in his bag instead.

The unsuspecting man woke up and reached the palace. There, as he pulled out his gift for the king, and lo and behold, what should he find! He was shocked and disappointed. As he was wondering how this happened, Kalidas, the court poet, did some quick thinking and said to the king:

'Khandava forest was burnt by Arjuna
Lanka was set fire to by Hanuman
Kamdev was burnt by Shankar
But nobody was able to burn poverty
Which burns everyone.
You alone are capable of doing so.'

Thus, the poor man was saved from humiliation and poverty. But poverty still awaits complete annihilation.

A poor man is never envied, poverty has never been considered desirable, the poor have always been exploited. How do we change the situation?

The contribution of economics

Modern economics believes in self-motivation—the motivation of self-interest. That every person should enhance his self-interest as much as possible and earn as much wealth as he can. That self-interest is directly proportional to economic development. I do not think there is no truth in this statement. I agree that nothing else can get a job done as much as self-motivation and self-interest. The self is very attractive, and we love ourselves so much that we will go to any extent for our interests. So, this theory of economics for development is attractive and desirable: to accumulate as much as you can.

If this is the capitalistic view, the communists promise that no one will be left hungry or without shelter, clothing or employment. This promise was an attractive dream and has remained one.

Attractive versus beneficial

In this context, if we see what Mahavira has said, we need to begin by understanding the difference between that which is attractive and that which is beneficial. Something may be attractive but not beneficial and something else may be beneficial but not attractive. Of course, there may be certain things which are both attractive and beneficial.

That every person should become rich, where self-interest grows enormously and there is great multiplication of wealth is an attractive idea but not necessarily beneficial. At all times, self-interest is one of the most dominant expressions of mankind. Being so, if it is linked with economic prosperity then many problems crop up. When self-interest is promoted without discretion, we have the situation as we are faced with today—violence and greed—and all that remains is self-interest with no concern for the other.

Everyone wishes economic development, but how should it be? What should be the route?

Mahavira says when we talk of economic development, the following points must be kept in mind: one, the means for earning wealth should be pure; two, it should be non-violent; three, moral values should be upheld; and four, there should be limits to self-interest.

Non-violence and pure means of production

Are we fostering violence along with economic development? Let us look at it from the means of productions we use:

Economic development must take place but not in an unchecked manner. An ordinary man robs a rich man. Now he has become wealthy. Is this development? Is the method employed by him correct? Can he be an example?

In ancient times, it was said that fame is equal to victory. Once an ordinary man thought of becoming famous. So, people gave him terrible suggestions, as summarized in an oft-quoted Sanskrit verse:

> *Ghatam bhindyat patam chindyat kuryat rasabharohanam*
> *yena kena prakarena prasiddhah purusho bhavet*

> Break a pot, tear away your clothes, ride a donkey if you please
> But in whatever way, become a man of fame.

No development can be truly so if it tramples upon the ethical values of society. Only that development is sustainable which rests firmly on the right means.

At this point it may be relevant to compare the two ideas of fame and greatness.

Everyone aspires for fame as it is understood as being synonymous with success. Fame can be for good or bad reasons. A person can become famous or infamous.

Fame has to be for the right reasons and well-earned through action and reputation, not through publicity and stunts. The fame that comes from within is greatness. And that is our goal. Mahavira says anything earned with ethical values will bring greatness in its wake for it does not stop with improving self-image in the public eye but also improves one from within.

In the kind of society envisaged by Mahavira, development of the economy goes hand in hand with the development of compassion and humane sensibilities. It should not be that with success and development we lose our compassion and kindness. One man may become wealthy collecting riches by exploiting many—but what about the thousands who could not make any progress in their lives because of this man's exploitation? This is a crucial point for those aspiring to greatness and success: it is not achieved by exploiting others nor by losing our intrinsic humanity. Fame is now as instant as instant food. Greatness takes time and demands integrity of character.

Limits to self-interest

To a certain extent, selfishness is present in everyone. Even the one who meditates does so with some motivation for the betterment of the self. This is not all bad or undesirable. But there has to be a limit to self-serving. It should not be at the cost of others. We are not alone in this world. There are millions of others. Economic development should not be such that we alone benefit from the exploitation of others, by causing harm to many.

Dharma and economic development

Dharma, or, roughly speaking, religion, does not present any obstacles to economic growth. Many modern economists talk of the barriers that religion presented, which hampered economic development. But such restrictions only impede development when we look at it from the perspective of what we like, not from that which is beneficial. If you look at it from the perspective of that which is beneficial, then the speed breakers instituted by religion along the path of economic development prove supportive to it, not detrimental. Small things make a difference. Take the ideal of *aparigraha*, for example. *Aparigraha* means not accumulating possessions, be they thoughts or material. To not cling to one's thoughts and allow others also to give their opinions will definitely make a better place to live in. For businessmen, to not hoard is good advice. If economics takes into consideration that which is pleasant and that which is beneficial, then it can truly help us. Today's economics, by and large, looks only at that which is pleasant or nice in the short term but ignores the long-term implications, which has given rise to many problems. For example, we need to pay more emphasis to education. That will build a better nation tomorrow even if it takes away from our budgets now. The well-lit billboards that we spend so much on may look modern and make the city landscape attractive, but in the long run, education is in the greater interest of the people and so should be our focus.

The technological perspective

No doubt, we have made progress in the field of technology. We have benefitted greatly from the progress. But if compassion had also grown with it, it would perhaps not present such a danger to humanity. It is commonplace to comment on how hundreds of people walk side by side, but none of them look around to see the other because each one is on the phone. I hear people tell me children in many countries seek the company of machines which talk to them and answer their questions. They have to do so because they lack human company. Our families have become small and unitary. Our reliance on technology is increasing. Artificial intelligence is taking over many of man's routine tasks, including in the hospitality and medical sectors. In today's world of artificial intelligence, where machines are poised to do everything, we have to retain our integrity. Or else, we may create an irreparable and irreversible situation.

Technology has progressed so rapidly towards destructive actions but not so much towards beneficial actions. In olden times, the aim was to keep expanding one's empire. Today, the world is dictated by economics. It is no longer a question of how much land you own or how vast your empire is. The deciding factor is how prosperous your economy is; Japan is an example.

Selfishness and cruelty

All nations are fighting to establish their economic supremacy and they have used technology effectively to that end. However, the same has not been done for economic upliftment. The argument is that with great industrial expansion, more opportunities, and therefore more employment, will be born. Compassion does not figure here. Where the self reigns supreme, compassion cannot find a place. Mahavira's firm conviction was that with an increase in selfishness, cruelty will increase too. If selfishness is checked, compassion will flourish. It is not possible for selfishness and compassion to peak simultaneously.

As Mahatma Gandhi had observed, man will never be able to achieve the objective of economic equality because individual capabilities and competencies are different. Thus, everyone cannot reach the same point. The consequence of allowing self-interest to dominate has been that wealth is concentrated in a few hands. So, all we have gained is a list—a list of the richest people around the world.

Along with this, we also have some thoughts on good standards of living which has brought many material products in its ambit. These products keep changing and we are ever in the run to maintain or achieve that lifestyle.

If the objective was limited to the satisfaction of basic needs, there would perhaps be no problem, as that would be a part of healthy thinking. But this concept of 'standard of living' has made basic needs a secondary issue and the craving for non-basic articles has been encouraged in people.

The three yardsticks of Mahavira

Mahavira has studied human nature and come to the conclusion that each person is different, and everyone cannot be measured on the same scale. He categorized people as those with—

1. many desires,
2. few desires,
3. no desires.

The one with many desires has naturally no time for human values. His pursuit of wealth transgresses all humane values. His selfishness knows no bounds. Therefore, Mahavira says, he will go to any extreme to get what he wants.

A case in point is the cruelty to animals to satisfy human needs. For instance, luxury goods and cosmetics use animal-derived ingredients and yet their demands keep increasing.

It is indeed difficult to visualize how, having expanded wants and built images of acquisition, we can be saved from such avarice. It is imperative to think of welfare even while craving for a product that gives pleasure. Without controlling wants and limiting desires, we cannot achieve welfare.

The one with limited desires does not negate the attraction of the material world but is not obsessed by it. This is the kind of economy Gandhi advocated. Mahavira called these people: *Dhammenna Vitthe kampanne*—those who can take dharma and vocation side by side. This person does not have to earn more to buy the latest watch or pay the mortgage for a palatial house. He or she is not under pressure and so frees the mind.

I would like to relate another story of Srimad Rajchand, a great follower of Jainism and the philosopher–advisor to Gandhi. Once, a man he had lent money to incurred heavy losses. He came to him and promised to return the amount he owed in time. 'But as of now, I am unable to do so,' he pleaded. Rajchand asked for their agreement papers. The man did not want to get the papers because he thought Rajchand would take him to court. So, he dilly-dallied. Finally, unable to put it off any longer, he produced the agreement. Rajchand tore up the document and said, 'Let us nullify that transaction.'

This is compassion. This shows that there is good in the world. This is also why the story of Rajchand is narrated again and again while the story of the men to who took their debtors to court remains buried in dusty court files, forgotten.

There is not a human being who has no desires. Monks and renunciates can only have less or little desire.

Here we come to the core of the issue we are faced with on a daily basis: are we buying things for our need or are we pandering our wants? If we pause to think about this, we will realize that our needs are limited. We can be perfectly happy with a certain number of possessions. It is our wants that are unlimited. We can never fulfil our wants. In the race to get all that we desire, we end up gathering more work, more stress, more disappointments and more depression. Like a bottomless pit, we will never be satiated. Instead, we will live in a clutter of material possessions.

If we live by our needs, we will have no provocation to exploit, cheat, bear ill will towards or feel jealous of another. We will have room for compassion and for the greatness we are striving for.

Economics, which is limited to economic growth, is not good enough. A synthesis of material prosperity and promotion of non-violence is essential today.

In their harmony lies our greatness.

17
Be Creative!

In Chapter 11, we moved inwards towards the stillness of our core and reasoned why it was important. Now, time has come for a spiritual adventure. Finding the core is essential to be creative, to let yourself be free, to make a new world for yourself and others. Conquer the aggression of the immediate. Look at becoming from being—like a light that ends darkness even when the sun has set.

Night had fallen; my room was lit by an electric lamp. There was a power cut, but within minutes electricity had been restored and the room was lit again. In this brief period of darkness, I thought, light is not natural. Darkness is. There is no powerhouse to generate darkness whereas there is one for light. There is also a transmission system for light, such as the lamp in my room. I thought, once again, how man craves that which is not natural. Take the case of forgiveness and anger. It needs extreme striving to inculcate forgiveness while the latter is spontaneously generated. Is not anger then natural and forgiveness unnatural?

I further introspected. As a monk, I am used to giving religious discourses and every time I ask my followers to cultivate forgiveness and eschew anger. I have discoursed on this theme many times, but to no avail—humans are still more prone to anger than to forgiveness.

I came across a man who had excessive fear. He used to be afraid of not just his immediate situation but also imagined ones. Even when he was alive and healthy, he would get worked up thinking about his death. All my sermonizing and persuasion failed. So, once again, I concluded that fear is natural and fearlessness unnatural.

In the story of Indian religions, there have been many sages who have challenged the lure of lust. We also know that none could truly conquer it. The rigorous self-control and its sustained practice so essential for sexual control would lead anyone to infer that it is unnatural.

With all these thoughts assailing my mind, I was completely out of my depth. How is it that the emotions we feel naturally inclined towards we regard as undesirable and those that we are reluctant about we regard as desirable?

We have a natural liking for things we feel a need for, as in the case of food and water. No one has placed an embargo on them. Further, if I were to ask, if you ever felt the need for religion; if you felt miserable in its absence, or, if its absence handicapped you in any way, the answer would be obvious. If the need for it were as imperative and obvious as that for food and water, there would be no need to bind people to follow a religion. Only the demands of the body and heart are natural.

It is well known that the union of physical and emotional needs characterize life. In other words, life can be defined as the fulfilment of natural needs. Can religion be a part of its definition?

All this leads me to believe that notwithstanding the Herculean efforts, made by countless people across the world over the centuries to turn the natural into the unnatural, nothing has been achieved. Physical appetites and urges are even today as compulsive as in the past (chronologically or evolutionarily). We are irrevocably wedded to exhibiting hatred and anger and opposed to peace, love or genial conduct.

Shall we then admit the futility of light? The helplessness of the sun against darkness? Obviously not.

One evening, at sunset, the sky was overcast. The pitter-patter of rain soon gave way to a thunderous storm, with flashes of lightning. And it even hailed. I noticed a monkey on a tree, not too close by, shivering in the cold. I started thinking, man too must have lived similarly and would continue to do so if not for his inventiveness and courage. A creative man has always posed a challenge to the vacuity of nature. The skyscrapers symbolize his victory over nature.

A man went to visit his sister, and she invited him to stay on for lunch. He sat down for the meal with her family. The dishes were laid out on plates and covered with napkins. As the napkins were lifted, they revealed exotic preparations of great variety. When the brother's plate came, it looked just like anyone else's at the table. But he was in for a shock. He lifted the napkin to find a heap of wheat grain, some salt, sugar, spices, rice grains and so on. The sister burst out laughing watching her brother's face. 'Nature's gift, as it is,' she murmured.

A few months later, when her daughter was engaged to be married, the sister wrote to her brother informing him of the happy event. It was customary for brothers to send gifts. Soon, carts after carts arrived. The excited sister called the whole village to open the presents. When they did finally unpack the carts, they contained bales and bales of cotton. 'Nature's gift, as it is,' said the brother in his note.

Another incident that set me thinking was quite different. I saw a young woman boiling milk over a stove. Every time the temperature rose and the milk was about to boil over, she sprinkled water to settle it. This indicated that man seems to be constantly challenging nature—in this case, the simple process of diffusing the heat. Does that mean his courage and creativity cannot be kindled without challenging that which is natural? My inner voice reasoned: without such a challenge there would be no creativity.

Both the events reveal the same truth: only that is natural in this physical world which has not met with an intervention from man, not met with his creativity. In other words, it is creativity that divides being from becoming. To be human is to prefer becoming to being. That is why the eternal human refrain is to seek adventure, to be creative.

Once I was sitting on a seashore and watching the sea's inherent spirit in its fathomless depths. The undulating waves came right up to my shadow in the waters and then receded. Are sea waves not natural? Of course, they are, I thought. A sea without waves is like sunrise without daylight.

Similarly, it is impossible to concede the presence of emotions and deny the existence of sexual desire, anger and fear. A mere denial will not guarantee spiritual exaltation.

Let me relate yet another incident. I was sitting in one corner of a room, wrapped in a blanket. Icy winds from the north chilled the air. The newspaper in my hands announced the complete freezing up of the Arctic. My imagination rose and pointed out that there were no waves in frozen water. Does that mean the basic nature of the ocean had undergone a change? If I accepted that, would I get closer to the truth? Should I liken the body to the ocean and the passions of sex, anger and fear to its waves and say that the freezing of the former has resulted in the cessation of the latter? In fact, these phenomena are but two styles of stating the same truth. With the intensification of concentration on the centre of the inner being, 'endo-centring', passions calm down and eventually bow out. At this point, I am not going to discuss the process but am merely hinting at the fact that man's courage and creativity are inherent in his ability to change that which is natural and thus the eternal human refrain.

It is in this adventure that man's greatness lies. An enlightened and morally valorous person is never satisfied with just 'being' and is always actively pursuing 'becoming'. The change of the natural into the unnatural and vice versa is due to this creative effort.

Such an adventure brings about a change in the world of consciousness. If we predicate naturalness to what is, that is, being, our development will be hindered. With development, the context and relative norms of what is natural also change. By embarking on such a course of development, man overcomes the aggression of the immediatc and heads towards understanding the remote and the invisible. Ultimately, he can reach a stage where his real nature is revealed to him.

Then his understanding of what is natural changes. It is this self-realization—the direct comprehension of reality—that becomes an everlasting experience.

18
The Spiritual Point

Be creative! Seek adventure!

What is spirituality? The experience of freedom.
What is spirituality? The experience of completeness.
What is spirituality? The experience of being blessed.

Such a free, complete and blessed spirit is a creative one. It looks beyond the 'aggression of the present' to envision a wide canvas—the whole Universe waiting to be understood, interpreted. Spirituality means widening your canvas—getting rid of I and Mine and seeing the whole world as one.

One edge of imagination
Is in your hands
And the other, in mine.
They could embrace
Or, from each other, move away

Savvasim jiviyam piyam: To each and every being, life is dear.

I am acquainted with the truth that space is infinite. Yet, I have been trying to confine it. I have confined space and call it my home. Another confined space is the one I call office. My home has space, but space is not limited to it. It gives me refuge, shelters me from the vagaries of the weather, and so I call it mine and protect it. Every man's home is precious to him. I have no right to think there is none of that infinite space in another man's house. Every individual has confined a part of the collective infinite space to call it his home. That is to say, we are all drawing from the same common space and then naming it as mine and his or hers. The moment we break the boundaries in our minds we give up a sense of 'mineness'. That is not to say we break down the walls of our house, it is just to suggest we break the mental boundaries that divide us. Equally, if we can be as concerned about protecting the other person's space as we are about protecting our own, we are looking at the whole world as one. That is the meaning of the famous Sanskrit aphorism, *vasudaiva kutumbakam*—the whole world is one family. That is the spiritual point.

Abandonment of mineness results in its extension and extension of mineness results in its abandonment. Mineness imposes kinship on the non-kin. It is reflected in expressions like 'my house', 'my family' and so on. Injustice and exploitation are nursed by this discrimination because of what we think is ours. The process of abandonment is itself the process of extension. Give up the feeling 'this is mine' and treat everyone as yours.

This expanded area of 'yours' becomes your workspace, the space to have a sense of belonging to, to practice your compassion, to show your concern for humanity.

Man builds his house by enclosing a little space from infinite space. He illuminates it with portions of sun's infinite rays. So too is the human body housing the infinite and eternal soul. Even though we cannot see the soul, just as we see the sun entering our house through closed windows, every living being has a soul. We need to respect that.

All those who have gotten close to Truth are those who have tried to see it factually and objectively.

Anyone engaged in the quest for truth is spiritual. Curious to know the truth, man investigates and follows it—that is a spiritually inclined or spiritual person.

Sampikkhae appagamappaenam: See yourself through yourself.

Let us see and think. When we see we are unable to think, and when we think we are unable to see. When our mind is without thoughts, we are able to see; when we see, our mind becomes automatically free of thoughts. Thought restraint has a formula: seeing. Seeing needs no language. Thinking does. Limitation of language sets the two apart. Seeing intensely is concentration. Whether we look afar or near, whether we look into the body or at external objects, everything relates to the present. We can see neither the past nor the future.

Today, it seems like the whole world is afflicted with problems, problems of many kinds. It looks as though a play is being staged. In it the seer and the scene seem to emerge together. There seems no difference between the one who is seeing and the scene that is being enacted. There is complete identification of the seer with the scene. This is what we call a state of deep sleep.

When the one who sees awakens, the problems will solve themselves. All we need to do is to define the relationship between the one who sees and the scene. It will be an unnatural relationship if the one who sees forgets his existence in experiencing the scene. This is where problems lie, this is the root cause. The harmonious relationship between the two comprises the blending of the seer's experience of his own self with that of the scene. That is when the seer is aware of his separate existence and yet is able to identify or experience a oneness with the scene he is seeing, then there is harmony. When the seer and the scene are disunited, whatever man sees he does not do and whatever he does not see. This is a deceitful state. In this state seeing and doing are divorced from each other. When the seer and the scene are united, man does only what he sees and sees only what he does. This is a morally upright state. In this state, moral rectitude and integrity are maintained.

There once lived a king who called for a painting competition. The participants were to paint cocks and hens within a fixed period of time. The best painters took part in the contest. The allotted time came to an end and the paintings were brought in for review. The most famous painter of the area had not sent in his work. The king sent his emissary to find out why. The king's men could not find the painter anywhere. Finally, they located him in a coop. He asked for more time. That time was also over. The painter finally submitted his work. All the paintings were then exhibited. Judging them was difficult. So, they brought in cocks and hens from the king's poultry farm. They all went straight to the last painter's canvas and started pecking at it—it looked the most real. 'I spent a month in the coop to be able to paint it. I had to feel like one of them,' the award-winning painter said.

The story is an illustration of the idea that the painter was seeing and aware of his separate existence and saw the birds in the coop. He was able to recreate them because he experienced oneness with them. His complete concentration was on them. He did not forget he was a painter and that is why he observed them so well that he could paint them.

In any situation that you find yourself in, define your role, observe what you see and then act. Neither are you the situation itself nor are you unrelated to the situation. Problems have to be addressed. When emotions take prominence, the situation and the seer become one. To keep them separate is key.

Parasparaopagraho jivanam: Life is based on mutual support and interdependence.

The attitude

O Sun! you are the soul of light. The whole earth is illumined by you. Darkness disappears.

You are the awakening of the soul. When you rise, people wake up too.

You are the soul of fearlessness. With your appearance people open their house doors. Fear disappears.

You are the energizer. With your appearance, the whole sky is filled with birds and the streets with people. Inactivity is transformed into activity.

Darkness complains that
The sun is chasing it.
But the sun does not know
What is darkness.
The ignorant complains
Consciousness is chasing him.
Consciousness does not know
What is ignorance.

Even then, I do not like you, the reason being you want to shine alone by outshining or covering with darkness all other celestial objects. How can such an entity be likeable? The sun wants to shine alone. Is he cruel?

Anyone who wants to possess everything without sharing cannot but be cruel. Non-violence is linked to non-possession.

To come too close
To too bright a light
Is not good
To say this
The stars of the day
Are very eager
But the light of the sun
Even for two seconds
Is not willing to unveil them.

So, I feel, only that individual who lacks the sense of non-violence or equality will be drawn to possessions and possessiveness. Here, possession refers to hoarding and accumulation, not to meetings one's needs. Possessions may also be in terms of ideas and beliefs, to which one is overly attached.

Hold on to the minimum. Share the maximum, for life is based on mutual support and interdependence.

We are also drawing support from the world around us as we have seen how interdependent we all are. Interesting that is why we are all a little 'imperfect'.

The joy of imperfections

If man were perfect where would there be space for human effort? Fuel is essential for fire. Hunger is essential for a person to work. People wake up because they have to work and earn their livelihood. Workers wake up early because they have to report at work. Teachers wake up early because they have to go to school and teach. Likewise, every individual gets up in order to do his or her job. If people became perfect, they would idle away their time. Human effort has its basis in imperfection. Real joy lies in remaining imperfect, not in perfection. Leave perfection to God, for human beings only imperfection is desirable. If there had been no imperfection, no community would be formed. For instance, when we speak, whom do we speak to? We need a listener. Only then our speech has any meaning to it. We need each other's support and that is why we get into relationships of different kinds.

It is surprising that even though man is dependent on the external world, he always talks in terms of the perfect and the absolute. He boasts of a house worth a million rupees but is not worried about the dirty drain outside or the slum behind his house. How long will he remain unaffected by the poisonous fumes from the drain or the rising discontent of the slum dwellers? Nowadays people tend to live very insular lives. The virtual world is one reason. The second is the constant desire for comfort, which keeps a person from mingling with the general people, be it for reasons of heat, dust, pollution or anything similar. This distances him from his neighbours, friends and family. But can anyone, who by nature is imperfect, survive by severing his relations with the world? You cannot be an island. We have to help/support and receive help/support.

Appana sachchamesejja: Seek your truth yourself.

Liberation

The self is the lamp of consciousness, not the body. The self is the storehouse of purity. The objective of carrying the body is to ensure that the lamp of consciousness remains alight and the storehouse of purity remains full. If the object is defeated, if the lamp is extinguished (if we no longer listen to our consciousness), the storehouse is emptied (that is, more negative karmic debts incurred), the limits of carrying the body are automatically transgressed. To keep the lamp burning and to fill the storehouse is to find the exit from the cycle of life and death.

Living, I am in the consciousness
Burning the lamp of immortality
Pulsating to stillness, I am
Whether the breath comes or not.

Part 2

On Jainism and Preksha Dhyan

1
What Is Jainism?

I was once asked what is special about my religion that cannot be found in others. I replied, 'It is difficult to say what is special about any religion. Jaina philosophy and religion are gifted with the perspective of anekanta through which we see the rest of the world. This is a rare gift. This teaches me not to regard any philosophy or religion as espousing the absolute truth. Everything is therefore relative.'

The sixth century BCE was an epoch-making time as far as the quest for Truth was concerned. A number of legendary philosophers such as Mahavira and Buddha in India, Lao-tse and Confucius in China, and Pythagoras in Greece had been born in this century. They lived in different parts of the world, but their quest led them towards the same eternal Truth, which is not conditioned by any particular space or time. Mahavira was not the founder of Jainism but one who gave it new life, the one who resurrected it. He was the twenty-fourth Tirthankara or ford-maker in the Jaina tradition. A Tirthankara is one who after finding enlightenment returns to the people to guide them on the spiritual path.

The basic tenets of religion preached by Mahavira can be divided into *tattva, dharma* and *vyavahara*. The philosophy based on his teachings follows the following main principles: anekanta, ahimsa (non-violence), *aparigraha* (non-possessiveness) and *paurusha* (self-exertion). His teachings aimed at binding knowledge to action. Jainism does not believe in a creator, but that knowledge is acquired by one's own experience or through pure perception. Mahavira emphasized on experience, urging every individual to attain self-perfection, which, in the real sense, is the God within. He said, 'Truth has to be self-sought, it is one's perception and understanding. Written scriptures cannot be the last word.'

Since the dawn of time the question 'What is truth?' has plagued humanity and been debated upon. An earthen pot may, due to any given reason, break and become one with the earth. So, what is the true state of it—pot or clay?

Jaina philosophers suggest we look at the two states, not in a fragmented way but as an integrated whole, which is possible only through anekanta—the multifaceted point of view. There are two ways to look at anything: *dravyarthika* or the substantial, and *paryarthika* or the modal. *Dravyarthika* describes the matter that an object is made of. *Paryarthika* describes the shape or form it is in at any given point. The first is the transcendental view or *nischaya drishti*, and the second is the empirical view or the *vyavahara drishti*. When we look at an object from these perspectives, we find that the *parmanu* or the smallest indivisible particle of both pot and clay is the same. It is only the form that has changed. Jainas refer to matter as *pudgala*. So *pudgala* is the same while the form is variable. Both coexist.

There are three aspects to this: creation, cessation and permanence. Jainas correlate this to three activities that define life: *pravritti*, *nivritti* and *tatashta*. *Pravritti* is outward action, *nivritti* is inward repose and *tatashta* is the unchanging or the permanent.

We do an activity to attain happiness. We abstain from an activity that is painful and remain neutral if an activity causes neither pleasure nor pain, that is to say we do it or do not do it with detachment—not expecting pleasure or pain.

Three people went to a goldsmith. One wished to buy a crown, another a jar and the third pure gold in whichever form. They found the goldsmith melting a golden jar to make a crown. The first person was happy since a crown was getting made. The person who wanted to buy a jar was unhappy and the third one was neither happy nor sad, since he wanted only gold and that he could get, be it in the form of a crown or a biscuit.

Our world is interlinked. No object or being is completely different from another. At a gross level, we can see how one person is related to different people in different ways; a daughter to one, a wife to another, a mother to someone and so on. If you investigate the subtle world, the interconnectedness becomes even more intense. When something appears white in colour, a closer look reveals that it is actually made of seven colours. To extend this discussion into the realm of human affairs, let me talk about the next belief of Jainism—the existence of the soul.

Jainism believes in the existence of the soul. It not only believes in its existence but has also described its nature and properties in detail. According to the *Acharanga Sutra*, the most ancient text of the Jainas, Mahavira said, 'The soul is the one that knows.' Another definition is, 'The soul is that through which one knows.' The *Acharanga Sutra* further states, *savve sara niyattanti*, or all expressions fail to describe it. The soul is called *ajneya* or beyond the mind's comprehension, which is indescribable in words.

A liberated soul has no form, colour or smell and is not attached in any one place. It is pure consciousness. The nature of the soul is reincarnative, but many people do not know who they were in their previous birth or who they will be in the next. The soul is eternal or *trikalika*. Each one of us has a distinct soul that carries forward to its next birth its *tejas sharira* (bio-electrical body) and the *karmana sharira* (the subtle-most body).

There are many who are sceptical about rebirth. But Jainism is a scientific religion and let me explain why.

The present age is the age of science. You might say, it is easy to claim that for Jainism too. But it is not with that arrogance that I speak. I speak of Jainism as a scientific religion based on the scientific enquiry of truth that it unfolds.

Human being above all texts

The scientific nature of the Jaina's enquiry into truth is seen in the very basic sutra: *Appana sachchamesejja*, that is, search for truth yourself. Jaina philosophy does not believe that truth was revealed by some indescribable power. Every individual who undertakes penance for the quest for truth has the opportunity of arriving at it. The human being is an attestation of the truth—the loudest attestation. He is the scripture and the teachings.

Mahavira established the primacy of the human being over texts and teachings. The one who accepts this philosophy becomes a follower of the human being who sets an example, not of an outdated text.

Truth is infinite. Matter takes many forms. As a new form is created, the old one perishes. So, matter is never the same, it is constantly evolving. Every moment it takes on a new form; it has as many forms as the many moments it has gone through. We are constantly exploring matter and its different modes in order to understand the world. But to understand the nature of matter, which is transient, it is necessary to understand that which is eternal. Therefore, every individual can explore and understand the eternal or the truth.

The eternal and the transient

One person attains enlightenment. He knows truth in its entirety, and sees it in its fullness. And yet, his experience does not put an end to the quest for truth. That is because even though an enlightened person, *kevali*, as he is called, sees and knows the truth in its entirety, he is not able to express it in language. Our language is limited. Our expression is limited. So, truth as a whole can never be expressed. Therefore, the search continues.

Our world is constantly changing. Our society is too. The Jaina philosophy states that the changing and the constant are two aspects of truth. That philosophy which can define the changing without reference to the constant, or the constant without reference to the changing, is not scientific. The concept of anekanta embraces the ideas of the changing and the constant, or the transient and the eternal, equally and respects that one cannot be without the other.

The material world as real

Jaina philosophy accepts the existence of both sentient and the insentient as having independent existence in the world. *Jiva* or the soul is sentient. In this context, I am using *pudgala* to mean the physical existence of matter. The question is: what is the inter relationship between *jiva* and *pudgala*? *Pudgala* is also called *ajiva*, or that which is without *jiva*. So our question, in other words, is what is the relationship between that which is possessed of consciousness and that which is not? Jaina thought believes they cannot be independent of each other because they not only coexist but intermingle with each other. When *jiva* and *ajiva* come together, they create vital energy. It is *jiva* which breathes, takes in energy etc. Neither the *jiva* nor pudgala can exist alone.

Vedanta recognizes only the 'conscious' element while the Charavakas recognize only the material world. Jaina philosophy recognizes the independent existence of both the living and the non-living, both *jiva* and *ajiva*.

When the two ingredients get together, the energy their interaction generates is known as *vyanjana paryaya*. *Paryayas* or transformations are of two kinds: *svabhava* or natural and *vyanjana* or unnatural or synthetic. The former creates new shapes out of transformation from within itself while the latter occurs due to the interplay of different substances. For example, water is the result of interaction between hydrogen and oxygen, it is not a basic substance by itself.

We see the world evolving every moment. This expression manifests itself in varied forms, colours and shapes. This is due to the *vyanjana paryaya* or *jiva* and *ajiva*.

According to Jaina philosophy, the world has neither a beginning nor an end. *Jiva* or the soul has no image, it cannot be seen. To deny its existence because it has no form and is not visible is not justified, they say.

Individual accountability

Another aspect of the scientific nature of the quest for truth in Jaina thought is that it does not give leave of reason because of some higher power or circumstance. It insists on the individual taking responsibility for his actions. It brings accountability. One cannot say, 'What can I do? The circumstances were such.' Or, 'This is how God willed it.' The feeling that the all-pervasive God controls everything has belittled the power of and need for moral rectitude in people. Till a person takes responsibility for their actions, their own consciousness cannot develop. And that is the need of the hour—to awaken individual consciousness. In its absence mental illusions crowd and confuse the mind. To live in this confusion is to get lost in the labyrinth of the world, to lose yourself.

Karma

The belief in karma is another touchstone of the nature of any religion. Many religions accept a unidimensional aspect of the theory of karma as the root cause for anything that comes to be, turning human beings into mindless puppets. This is not desirable. Karma is a truth that influences the consciousness of a person. It is not be the be-all and end-all. Factors like time, nature, effort and fate also influence man's consciousness. The consciousness is sometimes influenced and sometimes not. If it were always influenced by one or the other, it would not have an independent identity of its own. Because it has the capacity to remain without being influenced, it retains its identity.

To be able to understand the multidimensional nature of the human being, we need to take a holistic approach. This kind of approach is scientific in nature for it takes everything into consideration. Relativity and contextual understanding are the distinguishing features of contemporary thinking. Through these the unfathomable depths of the ocean of the truth can be touched.

2
What Is Anekanta?

Anekanta is not a clever play of words. It is born of keen observation and deep reflection. For those who wish to trace its roots to Jaina philosophy, this chapter will be useful. Jaina philosophy contends that matter can neither be created nor destroyed. It just changes forms with a rearrangement of the molecules that make it. The variety we see in the world is but modifications of basic substances. Every substance has three distinct features: destruction, creation and the eternal.

The canonical literature (Agamas) of the Jainas form the basis of their philosophy. The word anekanta does not appear in the Agamas. It was probably first used by Siddhasena Divakara (500 BC–610 BC) who authored some of the significant texts on Jaina philosophy.

The basis of anekanta is *naya*, which could be translated as perspective. The *Bhagavati Sutra* deals with reality from two perspectives or *nayas*: the substantial (*dravyarthika*) and the modal (*paryayarthika*). The two viewpoints are relative, according to Acharya Siddhasena. Their relativity is known as anekanta.

The philosophical thoughts in India range from thoughts on absolute permanence to those on absolute transitoriness. The insentient element (*prakriti*), according to Sankhya philosophy, is permanent and transitory, but the sentient element (purusha) is absolute permanence, admitting no modifications. According to Vaishesika philosophy, the earth is permanent as cause and transitory as effect, but the soul, God and space are without any modification. According to Buddhist philosophy, reality is momentary—whatever is real is momentary, like a cloud. The concept of eternity is rejected outright in Buddhism. In Vedanta, Brahman is absolute and unchangeable and maya is changeable; Brahman is beyond reality and unreality—it is indescribable.

In the context of the above discussion, we can see how anekanta embraces both permanence and impermanence in its concept. Acharya Hemachandra puts this poetically in the verse:

> *Adipamavyomasamasvabhavam*
> *Syadvadmudranatibhedi vastu*
> *Tannityamevaaikamanityamanya-*
> *Diti tvadajnaadvistam pralapah*

> Just as a lamp's light is held within space, so too is the nature of reality held within the argument of *syadvada*. Some philosophers not acquainted with you, O lord, declare reality to be absolute permanence or absolute impermanence.
>
> —*Anyayogavyavachchedika*

From the viewpoint of substance, reality neither originates nor perishes. From the viewpoint of mode or forms, they originate and perish. The *Bhagavati Sutra* speaks of two aspects of reality: the permanent and the temporary. The permanent does not undergo change while the temporary does: *athire palottai, thire no palottai.*

Umaśwati, another great Jaina scholar who lived somewhere in the first four centuries, defined reality to be consisting of permanence, origination and destruction based on the twin perspectives of substance and mode—*utpadavyaayadhrauvya-yuktam sat* (*Tattvartha Sutra* 5/29).

Reality therefore has three characteristics and is called *anekantika* (multidimensional). One cannot comprehend reality without anekanta.

What does anekanta or non-absolutism mean?

Anekanta is lexically a negative term, but substantially it is not negative. Anekanta conveys the relation between substance and mode. It is not possible to have just one of them, that is, substance and mode cannot exist without each other. The very nature of reality being *anekantic* (multidimensional), *ekanta* (or of a single dimension) cannot be used to comprehend it. *Aneka* means more than one, not infinite or innumerable.

Modes are successive attributes. Infinite modes are not possible in a substance simultaneously, for they do not originate simultaneously.

An object is capable of undergoing infinite modifications. It is only on account of this capability that without giving up its own nature, it goes on transforming itself into various forms.

Reality *(sat)* and matter (*dravya*) are the objects of knowledge. *Naya, anekantavada* and *syadvada* are essentially forms of knowledge, or means to know. Sometimes we know wholly and sometimes part by part. The attempt to know the same reality through different ways forms the basis for *naya, syadvada* and *anekantavada*.

The doctrine of *naya* deals with the process of knowing reality, part by part. From the perspective of the object, the substantial *naya*, the substance is reality and its modes or forms are unreal. From *parayarthika naya,* or the perspective of modes, it is vice versa, that is, the modes are real and the object unreal.

The substantial viewpoint is the one from which we grasp the substance. Its modes are not part of this study, not that it denies the existence of modes. If the substantial denies the existence of modes, the viewpoint would become invalid, *durnaya*. Similarly, with the modal viewpoint. If either of them denies the existence of the other, they would become *aikanthika* or one-sided and hence invalid.

A one-sided view has created many problems in the field of philosophical thought. Anekanta provides a solution to them. If substantial or modal *nayas* were non-relative, anekanta would not exist. Reality has an innate capacity to change. Change is a part and parcel of reality. Permanence and change cannot be separated in totality, nor can they exist independently. It is to understand this fact: it is from their dependence and independence that non-absolutism rose.

What is syadvada?

Anekanta was born of the interdependence between substantial and modal viewpoints. *Syadvada* expresses that very interdependence. Anekanta works in the binaries of the permanent and the temporary, existence and non-existence, general and specific, one and many, expressible and the inexpressible. What unites these aspects is proved through *syadvada*.

Gautama, Mahavira's foremost disciple, once asked his teacher, 'Is the earth permanent or temporary?'

Mahavira answered, 'It is partly permanent and partly temporary.'

Syadvada accepts both the thesis and the antithesis. But how could the contradictory attributes of permanence and impermanence coexist?

Mahavira explains, 'The earth is permanent from the substantial point of view and temporary from the modal point of view.'

Saptabhangi

Existence has many modes. Three dimensions have been identified for determining the nature of each of these modes: existence, non-existence and inexpressibility. These three dimensions can express the nature of existence. A statement describing a flower as a rose is a positive statement. A statement saying the rose is not a datura flower is a negative. These two, together with a third statement which expresses the inexpressible, make for a complete description. The indescribable consists of unmanifested modes of matter or the molecules that form the rose today which it may take on in the future.

The doctrine of anekanta is not meant for contradicting other absolutist views. It is enunciated as a tool in the quest for truth. The nature of reality is explained through two perspectives, or *nayas*. By itself, the *naya* is absolutist. But anekanta adopts a relative absolutist view. Relativity is at the core of anekanta. In the Agama era, it was explained and discussed only to describe truth.

Mahavira said, 'Just as truth cannot be worded, it can also be worded. If it is unreal to accept that truth can be worded, it is equally unreal to think truth cannot be worded.'

Reality is obtained by bringing about a balance between these two options. Balance is defined as the coexistence of apparently opposing forces. In the material world, there is complete balance and coexistence. It is our intellect that has visualized opposites.

The following conversation between Mahavira and Gautama may make this clearer.

Gautama: 'Lord! What is truth?'

Mahavira: 'It cannot be told.'

'Then how do we know it?'

'You search for it yourself.'

'But how to search for it?'

'Give up karma, do not fill your mind with thoughts, keep silent and keep the body still.'

'Lord, how will there be life then?'

'Restrain your activities. Speak only if you have to. Walk only if you have to. Eat if you have to. Do everything but with restraint.'

'Lord, if the path to truth can be told why not truth itself?'

'This is a partial truth. Partial truth can be worded. I express relative truth. Complete truth can never be given expression. Therefore, I say truth cannot be expressed. Truth is expressible and inexpressible and a relative understanding of the two is the right knowledge.'

'Lord, what is expressible truth?'

'From the perspective of identity, existence (alone) is the truth and from the perspective of differences, substance and its modes are the truth. Substance is permanent. Modes are impermanent. The balance of the permanent and the impermanent is truth. When we look at the world as our object of learning, then the existence and the changes of the sentient and insentient beings in the three time zones is the truth. Its division is untruth.'

3

Preksha Dhyan: An Introduction

One cannot achieve any desired goal without awakening one's energies. So, I focussed on awakening my strengths. There are three forms of energy:

1. Physical energy
2. Mental energy
3. Emotional energy

For physical energy I chose asana and pranayama. *Bhujangasana*, *matsyasana*, *paschimottanasana*, *suptvajrasana*, *uttanapadasana*, *baddhapadmasana*, *halasana* and *sarvangasana*—these were the main asanas I practised.

Anulom-vilom, *sukshmabastrika*, *suptbastrika*, *ujjayi*, *nadishodhana*, *kevala rechana* and *kevala kumbhaka*—these were the main pranayamas I followed.

Concentration

I thought no great job can be achieved by mere physical strength. For that concentration, single-mindedness is very important. I did many practices for concentration. They became my experiences. I chose the practice of *manas chakshu*, which means seeing through the inner eye. I made some sutras or guidelines for it:

1. Whichever object is being meditated upon, a mental picture of that object is to be made.
2. Whichever verse is to be learnt by heart, that should be seen written clearly in the sky and the mind should read it from there.
3. Whichever book is being learnt by heart, every word should be picturized and drawn before one's eyes.
4. While doing *japa*, that is chanting, every letter should be picturized with its phonetic place. For example, when saying Arham, with the sound of 'a' the focus should be on the throat, with 'r' the focus should be on the crown, 'ha' should again find focus on the throat, and for 'm' the focus should be on the lips. Arham is a seed mantra.
5. If any other chant is used to meditate, even there the attention should be focussed on the letters.

Practice for purity of emotions

In Jaina *tattva vidya* there is a lot of discussion on purity of emotions. The conclusion drawn there is that man's actions are directed by his emotions. The mind does not have an independent place. It is a tool to express emotions. The world of emotions is subtle. The mind expresses the subtle working of the emotions in the gross world. This way of thinking inspired me to think more on the purity of emotions. Without purifying emotions, one cannot make much progress in meditation based simply on the mind. Negative emotions are greatly responsible for making the mind restless. When emotions are purified, negative emotions reduce and concentration increases.

The nasal tip: an important centre of breath

I have paid special attention to the respiratory system, centres of breath and *sushumna*. Then a question arose: Lord Mahavira used to focus his eye on the tip of the nose and meditate. Why? I got the answer from hatha yoga. The nose is an important centre of breath. As you focus the mind there, the breath becomes stable and the pulse becomes slower. To meditate on the nasal tip is a very good way of controlling breath and thereby improving concentration.

Kayotsarga

The practice of *kayotsarga* has a special place in the Jaina tradition of meditation. Two words are very significant: *samvara* and *nirjara*. From the perspective of meditation, *nirjara* can be understood to mean building different mental states, and *samvara* as the state beyond the mind.

In the opinion of many thinkers, the restlessness of the mind is the prime obstacle to meditation. From Jaina texts I learnt that restlessness of the mind is not the first obstacle. The first obstacle is the restlessness of the body. *Kayotsarga* and *kayotgupti* are practices to still the body. Once this is achieved the mind automatically starts becoming calmer. According to Jaina thought, all activity begins with the physical body. The physical body does not absorb external influences in its still state. The restlessness of the mind will automatically reduce in a still body.

Kayotsarga literally translates to rising above the body. In common parlance, it can be understood as relaxation of the body with complete awareness. According to Mahavira, 'relaxation relieves one from all sorrow'. *Kayotsarga* leads to relaxation. Relaxation is the process of awakening the consciousness and relieving oneself from stresses. It is a state of deep relaxation.

Our physical ailments are because of the rigidity in our muscles, which may even cause uneven flow of blood. *Kayotsarga* is an effective exercise for removing rigidity, stiffness and inflexibility in the body. Today's medicine says one of the causes of illness is that we accumulate stress in our body. If we could relieve ourselves of the stress, we would be healthier and avoid some constitutional problems. Ideally, *kayotsarga* should be practised every day before going to bed.

Nirjara or different mental states can take a practitioner to mid-level meditation but not any higher. Only the beyond-the-mind stage can take a practitioner to new heights. Once that is achieved one does not have to think of building different states of the mind; it happens by itself.

This Jaina system of meditation is called Preksha Dhyan.

Preksha Dhyan: the method

The one who wants to practice Preksha meditation begins by seeking initiation into it. To seek to be initiated into meditation means to present oneself for the practice of meditation. One has to be mentally prepared. Once that is achieved, the next step is to find the path of spiritual practice. The objective of Preksha Dhyan is to open the inner eye.

Typically, the meditation begins with the recitation of Arham, followed by the aphorism: *sampikkhae appagamaappaenam*, or to observe the soul through the soul. With this resolve being articulated, the practitioner is set to engage in the practical work of meditation involving a series of exercises:

- *Kayotsarga* (relaxation)
- *Antar yatra* (inner journey)
- *Dirgha swas preksha* (the perception of deep breathing)
- *Alom-vilom* (the perception of breathing through alternate nostrils)
- *Sharir preksha* (the perception of body)
- *Chaitanya kendra preksha* (the perception of psychic centres)
- *Leshya dhyana* (the perception of psychic colours)
- *Dhyana* (meditation and contemplation)

These exercises constitute the essential elements of Preksha Dhyan. Practising these with faith and determination can unlock the secrets of healthy and peaceful living.

Preksha Dhyan has many steps and may be difficult for everyone to follow regularly, but even the daily practice of *kayotsarga* alone can go a long way in building concentration and awakening dormant energies.

Kayotsarga

Anyone who wants to live with zest must, first, find something worth doing; determine one's aim. In my opinion, the ultimate goal is to create an auspicious or supportive environment around oneself. Life should go on smoothly, filled with a sense of well-being, without any obstruction or negativity. The most important exercise for this is *kayotsarga*. I have spoken of it earlier.

The first step

Kayotsarga, the first step in Preksha Dhyan, is relaxation, through which stability of the body is achieved. In this practice, the muscles are relieved from stress and relaxed by autosuggestion.

The practice of relaxation also constitutes the foundation for *anupreksha* (contemplation) and meditation. These are two important ways of bringing about a change in life.

Objectives of relaxation

- Realize that the soul and the body are two different entities.
- Reduce physical inertia.
- Hone intelligence.
- Develop the aptitude of enduring pain and pleasure with equanimity.
- Observe the subtleties of our inner body.
- Gain control over our emotions.

All these factors play an important role in the spiritual life and are of utmost importance for a practitioner. A renunciate is required to perform relaxation periodically.

In our present discussion, it is also an important step towards success in any venture, for it brings you back to yourself each time and therefore brings out the best in you.

Technique

There are four stages of *kayotsarga*:

- Stabilizing the body.
- Relieving all kinds of tension.
- Abandoning the gross body and coming closer to the subtle one.
- Realizing the soul's detachment from the body and that the soul and the body are two different entities.

For relaxation, select a quiet, clean and pleasant place. *Kayotsarga* can be done standing, sitting or lying down. In any of these postures, the body is to be kept calm and stable. The neck, spine/vertebral column and waist should be erect and upright but without stiffness, and the body should be left loose. Focusing on each part of the body, experience relaxation through autosuggestion. Relaxation is useful in providing relief from stress, tension and anxiety. Half an hour of relaxation can be equivalent to, and even more effective in, providing rest to the body than two hours of sleep.

All parts of the body should be still, like a sculpture. Relax and concentrate. Concentrate on the right toe, suggest it to relax and observe it relaxing. Similarly, focus on every part of the body, suggest its relaxation and experience the relaxation. And practise being still.

Relaxation can be practised for a long time in continuity or with breaks in between. In order to achieve different effects, one can practise it at different times of the day.

Duration

For improving physical and mental health, perform relaxation for twenty seconds to five minutes, several times a day.

- Begin any work with two minutes of relaxation.
- After finishing any task, practise relaxation for twenty minutes.
- For emotional well-being, practise relaxation for forty-five minutes, every day before lunch.

Benefits

- Relieves physical, mental and emotional stress.
- Soothes the nervous system.
- Slows down the rate of metabolism, breathing and heartbeats.
- Increases operational efficiency.
- Fixes insomnia.
- Helps to keep calm under any situation.
- Positive changes in the bio-electrical activities of the brain.
- Increases alertness, sharpens the intellect and concentration is achieved.
- Constant self-awareness leads to self-realization.

Preksha Dhyan: the steps in detail

Arham

Arham is a spell-word that augments the existing powers in us and around us. Different sounds have differing wavelengths and impact us in different ways. This combination unleashes our vital energy. In Jaina belief system, the word is the symbol of Mahavira and so gains even more significance. But the word itself is laden with energy:

'A' signifies the kundalini, or the luminous power,

'r' signifies fire; it destroys negative energy,

'ha' signifies space, it increases one's awareness of the supreme nature and purity of the all-knowing soul within one,

'm' is the reverberation which activates the sensory nerves.

Together, Arham becomes a very powerful chant.

An exercise

Focus your attention on the navel and visualize a golden lotus there. Recite Arham nine times, imagining that the golden rays from the lotus are permeating within. Suggest to yourself that no negative force can penetrate your armour created by Arham. This becomes a spiritual protection. The key is commitment to the sound and complete dedication to it.

Antar yatra

There exist two worlds—the external and the inner. We have a natural inclination towards the external world. This is because the senses are continually in touch with the external world. The mind too is more familiar with messages from the senses than impulses from the inner world. So, the inner world often remains unexplored because we are not acquainted with the powers that assist us in realizing its true beauty. In Preksha meditation, there is a technique called *antar yatra*, or the inner journey, through which one can become familiar with the inner world and realize oneself.

Objectives

- To initiate an upward movement of vital energy. The mind moves from *shakti kendra* (the centre of energy) towards the *gyan kendra* (the centre of knowledge).
- To cultivate the power of self-restraint.
- To boost vital energy.
- To create a strong platform for meditation.

The flow of consciousness in the central nervous system is part of the inner journey. The human nervous system comprises three subsystems:

- Parasympathetic nervous system (*ida*)
- Sympathetic nervous system (*pingla*)
- Central nervous system (*sushumna*)

The outward flow of vital energy is facilitated by the parasympathetic and sympathetic nervous systems. In terms of hatha yoga, these are synonyms for *ida* and *pingla*, respectively. For the inward flow, the consciousness must travel from *ida* and *pingla* towards the *sushumna* or the spinal cord.

Technique

In order to visit the inner world, one must withdraw one's attention from all external objects and focus on the centre of vital energy, situated at the base of the backbone or the vertebral column. Let the consciousness flow through the spinal cord, all the way from the centre of vital energy up to the centre of knowledge situated in the middle of the skull.

We can understand this process better through an example. Think of a well full of water. A man passes by and wants to fill a drum with it. He cannot reach the water below directly, so he ties a bucket to a rope. The bucket is lowered into the well, filled with water and then pulled out. By repeatedly filling and emptying the bucket, he can fetch the desired quantity of water to fill his drum. Similarly, our consciousness takes the shape of a bucket and our breath that of a rope to transport vital energy to the centre of knowledge, and vice versa. Synchronize one's internal trip with the process of breathing. During exhalation one should undertake the upward trip, whereas during the inhalation one should undertake the downward trip. It is essential to remain in the state of deep concentration during this exercise. Guided meditation sessions are essential to learn this seemingly simple technique.

Benefits

- Promotes physical well-being by strengthening the nervous system.
- Promotes mental well-being by revitalizing mental abilities.
- Promotes emotional well-being by establishing sustainable control over emotions.
- Promotes spiritual well-being by establishing efficient flow of vital energy.

- Sustained practice helps the practitioner to overcome anxiety and frustration of everyday life and assists in the awakening of supernatural powers.

Internal trip guides us to the unexplored zones of the subconscious, the tremendous source of positive energy that is hidden within us. It also strengthens the spiritual side of our life.

Perception of deep breathing

Our knowledge of breathing is limited and so is our understanding of it. To be able to look and travel inwards, it is important to keep pace with our breath. It is the greatest witness of our inner activity. For the right understanding of any action, we must know the movement of the breath at that time. Our breath is also our most important activity—to ignore it would not augur well for us, like the story of the hunter: a story which seem improbable, but the likes of which you may have encountered in your life too.

A hunter got down from his jeep in the middle of a forest. As he was exploring his surroundings, his eyes fell on a pair of eyes glimmering in a bush nearby. A lion soon showed itself. Ah, just his luck, for he had left his gun in the jeep. He had only stepped out for a moment and the lion chose that very moment to appear. 'I have the licence to shoot!' exclaimed the man, waving the piece of paper. The lion was not threatened by that.

Every cell in our body requires oxygen to function. What provides it with its essential resource? The breath. For our inner happiness, for the purity of our mind and our psychic well-being, it is necessary that the filth accumulated within us should be cleansed. Our body is activated by vital energy, whether of the body, mind or speech. It is our breath that fuels this vital energy. The art of breathing lies in taking fine breaths. The emphasis is on lengthening each breath. Through regular practice, we must reach a stage where we take only eight to ten breaths per minute. If we reach that stage, we can begin our inward journey. We may even reach a stage where we take just one or two breaths in a minute, and that will indeed be special.

- Regulate your breathing—make it slow, deep and rhythmic.
- Let the vibrations of each breath reach your navel.
- Allow your abdominal muscles to expand during inhalation and contract during exhalation.
- Concentrate fully on your navel. Practise deep, slow and rhythmic breathing by allowing each breath the same time. Perceive each inhalation and exhalation through the expansion and contraction of the abdominal muscles, respectively.
- Continuing the slow, deep and rhythmic breathing, shift your attention from the navel and focus it inside the nostrils at the junction of both the nostrils. Perceive each incoming and outgoing breath. Remain fully aware of each breath.
- Continuously practise slow, long and rhythmic breathing—inhale and exhale each breath while remaining fully aware of it.
- Fully occupy your mind with the perception of breathing.

- If you are distracted by any thought, do not try to stop it forcefully, but perceive it, and then again start perceiving your breath.
- If the distraction is frequent, you may hold your breath for a few seconds without causing any discomfort.
- Continue the awareness of breathing.
- Perceive it without any judgement.

Benefits of deep breathing include getting adequate oxygen for our body. Our morale improves. The mind becomes more vigorous and stable, and the endocrine glands function better. We have better control over our emotions. For example, when we get angry, our breath quickens. If we could slow down the pace of our breathing, we may not even get angry.

Deep breaths help us to live longer. The deeper and slower we breathe, the more we lengthen our life span.

Perception of alternate breathing

Breath is connected to the vital energy that runs through our body. Sometimes, this current runs through the left nostril and sometimes through the right. It is continually changing. According to ancient seers, it changes every two and a half quarters, one quarter lasting forty-eight minutes. Contemporary scientists say the breath changes every two and a half hours and is known as the nasal cycle. The study of the flow of breath through different nostrils is called *svar vigyan*. According to it, it is believed that breath should flow through the left nostril for calm and collected action. For fervent action it flows through the right. When breath flows through both the nostrils uniformly, it is optimal for deep meditation.

The cycle of the cerebral hemispheres

Along with the cycle of breathing, modern scientists also believe the hemispheres in the brain also function alternately, ninety minutes for the right and ninety minutes for the left. This does not mean the left hemisphere is inactive when the right is functioning, or vice versa; nor does it mean that the cycle of breathing and the cycle of the hemispheres interfere with each other. All it means is that, at any given point of time, one side is functioning more than the other.

In the practice of breathing through alternate nostrils, you have to inhale through one nostril and exhale through the other, switch the nostrils and repeat.

Try to accomplish the alternation by exercising your willpower.

In the beginning, you may make use of your finger and thumb for the alternate breathing technique. Place a thumb on your nostril and the ring finger of the same hand on the other nostril, and rest the middle and index fingers on the forehead.

Now, alternately remove the thumb and ring finger for the passage of breath through each nostril.

The third step for Preksha meditation is the perception of breathing through alternate nostrils.

- Regulate your breathing; make it slow, deep and rhythmic.
- Concentrate on the insides of your nostrils, practise breathing through alternate nostrils.

- Inhale through the right nostril and exhale through the left one.
- Now inhale through the left nostril and exhale through the right one; this completes one cycle.
- Repeat the same exercise; continue the rhythmic breathing.
- Perceive each inhalation and exhalation by concentrating the mind on alternate nostrils.
- Let your mind and breath go hand in hand.
- Do not think—no memory of the past, no imagination of the future.
- Simply perceive.

The mind should move with the breath.

While you are breathing in, let your attention follow the breath inside.

While you are breathing out, let your attention follow it outside.

Now, practise the perception of breathing through alternate nostrils together with holding the breath intermittently.

Concentrate your mind inside the nostrils.

- Inhale through the right nostril and hold the breath inside.
- Exhale through the left nostril and hold the breath outside.
- Again, inhale through the left nostril and hold the breath inside and exhale through the right nostril and hold the breath outside.

In this way, practise holding the breath four times during one cycle.

Continuously remain aware of each exhalation and inhalation.

You may hold the breath only for a few seconds without causing any discomfort.

Repeat the same exercise for several rounds.

Let the mind and breath go hand in hand.

In our day-to-day life, we experience the manifestation and coexistence of two opposing principles; for example, hot and cold, harmony and chaos, love and hate, good and evil, beauty and ugliness, constructive and destructive ideas, negative and positive attitudes, and so on. Under normal situations, these opposing forces remain in equilibrium. Similarly, our body maintains harmony between the two opposing subsystems of the autonomic nervous system that are responsible for our physical and psychological well-being. This harmony gets disturbed due to lifestyle changes.

Breathing can make a substantial difference in our life because breath remains connected and controls the working and harmony of the nervous system. We can breathe either through the right or the left nostrils, or through both of them. Breathing through alternate nostrils is an amazing phenomenon and the selection of the nostril largely governs the type of activities that one seeks to engage in. For example, fervid actions can be accomplished while breathing through the right nostril. In contrast, breathing through the left nostril imparts patience and perseverance. Similarly, breathing through both the nostrils takes us to the state of samadhi, a form of deep meditation.

Objectives

- To achieve and sustain a state of equanimity.
- To establish homeostasis in the body functions and processes.
- To gain higher levels of consciousness.

During the last millennium, scientific discoveries have revealed the secrets of the working strategies and the connection of the two cerebral hemispheres and the process of breathing. According to *Yogashastra*, the right hemisphere of the brain offers discipline, faith, friendliness, good conduct and other similar positive attributes, while the left hemisphere gifts logical and reasoning capabilities. Establishing balance between both hemispheres is the objective of alternate breathing.

For a spiritual life, equanimity is the founding principle. It is believed that the state of equanimity can be achieved by equally activating both the respiratory cycles. A more active right cycle causes aggression, anger, and tension while a more active left cycle leads to fear and inferiority complex.

While practising alternate breathing, mind and breath should accompany each other. Holding the breath also plays an important role in achieving the state of thoughtlessness.

Technique

First, inhale through the right nostril and hold the breath inside. Exhale through the left nostril and hold the breath outside. Second, inhale through the left nostril and hold the breath inside. Then exhale through the right nostril and hold the breath outside. It completes one round of alternate breathing. Regular practice can enhance concentration.

Benefits

- Higher levels of consciousness.
- Increases concentration and alertness.
- Provides extrasensory perceptions and intuition.
- Establishes homeostasis in the body functions and processes.

Perception of the body

The practice of the perception of body consists of concentrating the mind on each body part, one by one, and perceiving the sensations and vibrations taking place in each.

Here, the perception does not mean a visual perception, but a mental one.

The sensations may be superficial sensations of the skin such as contact with your clothes, warmth or coolness, itching and perspiration, or they may be the sensations of pain, numbness, tingling and so on felt in your muscles or the vibrations of electrical impulses in the nervous system or any other type of vibrations.

Starting from the surface, you have to penetrate deep inside and try to become aware of the internal and subtle vibrations.

Remain completely equanimous towards the sensations; try to keep your mind free from like or dislike.

This is the third step of Preksha meditation.

- Concentrate your mind on the big toe of your right foot. Allow it to spread and permeate throughout the whole portion of the toe. Perceive the sensations and vibrations taking place in that region. Become aware of them, experience them without any judgement; use deep concentration and remain fully alert.
- Now shift your attention to each part of right limb, one by one. I shall indicate the name of the part of your body on which you have to concentrate your mind and perceive it: the toes, the sole, the heel, the ankle, the upper part of the foot, the calf muscles, the knee, the thigh, up to the hip joint. Perceive the whole part, experience sensations and vibrations taking place in each. Maintain equanimity.
- In the same way, practice perception of all the parts of your left limb.
- Thus the trip of the lower body is completed.
- Then start the trip of the middle body from the waist up to the neck.
- Concentrating your mind on each part one by one, perceive the waist, the navel, the abdomen, including the big intestine, the small intestine, the kidney, the spleen, the liver, the pancreas, the duodenum, the stomach and the diaphragm. Then the whole portion of the chest, including the lungs, the heart, the ribs, the throat and the vocal cords. Concentrate your mind and perceive.
- Next, perceive the whole of your back, including the spine, the spinal cord and the neck.
- Concentrate on the whole portion of the right hand and arm, including the thumb, the finger, the palm, the wrist, the lower arm, the elbow, the upper arm and the shoulder.

Perceive each part one by one. In the same way, concentrate on the left hand and arm. The trip of the middle body is completed.

- Now we come to the upper body. Concentrate your mind on each part, from the chin up to the head. The chin, the lips, the inner portion of the mouth, including the tongue, the teeth, the palate, the cheeks, the nose, the right ear (all the three parts—the outer, the middle and the inner), the right temple, in the same way the left ear and the left temple, the right eye, the left eye, the forehead and the head. Perceive each part one by one. During the perception of the tongue allow your tongue to remain hanging freely, without touching anywhere inside the mouth.
- While perceiving the head, perceive all parts of your brain—the front, the back, the right, the left, the outer and the inner. Allow your mind to permeate throughout the brain. The trip of the upper body is completed.
- Now practise the perception of the body as a whole. You may stand up slowly and carefully, keeping your eyes closed. Allow your mind to travel from the big toes to the head and from the head to the big toes, quickly. Passing through each part of the body, perceive the vibrations throughout. Experience a tingling sensation in each muscle, skin, nerve and cell produced by the contact of your conscious mind. You may also practise holding the breath for a while intermittently. Get yourself completely absorbed in the perception of your body.
- Allow your mind to travel throughout the body, slowly. If you experience pain or any peculiar sensation, you may stop there for a while and perceive it with equanimity, without any like or dislike.

Perception of psychic centres

To make the psyche objective, to remove the bias created by the senses, we address the endocrines.

So far, we believed that the brain was the source of energy and the place from which the psychic forces acted. But now we know that it is only a repository of memories. The endocrine system is the seat of the impulses and emotions of an individual. The endocrine and the nervous systems are two very important parts of our body.

The following table shows the relation between the endocrines and the *chaitanya-kendras*:

Endocrines	*Chaitanya-kendra*
Pineal	*Jyoti-kendra*
Pituitary	*Darshana-kendra*
Thyroids	*Vishuddhi-kendra*
Thymus	*Ananda-kendra*
Adrenals	*Taijasa-kendra*
Gonads	*Svasthya-kendra* and *shakti-kendra*

Constant triggering and overaction of the lower endocrines, namely, adrenals and gonads, result in pernicious bad habits, affecting our physical and mental health.

Development of the upper endocrines alone can modify the synthesis of the endocrine output, and weaken the intensities of the primal drives, thus making them controllable. Constant and regular practise of *chaitanya kendra preksha* results in establishing a firm control of the reasoning mind over all actions which would ultimately bring about the desirable transformation in mental behaviour and habits.

Shvasa preksha, *sharira preksha* and *chaitanya-kendra preksha* are tools for developing the powers of a reasoning mind. Once authority over the fully developed reasoning mind is established, it would prevent the recurrence of old injurious habits.

Practice *chaitanya-kendra preksha* for thirty minutes. The soundtrack can be played from this URL: https://www.youtube.com/watch?v=yt1211EEtW0

Choose an asana (posture) that is convenient: *vajrasana*, *padmasana* or *ardhapadmasana*. Adopt the *dhyana* mudra. Sit straight. Repeat Arham.

Sampikhaye appaga mappayenam

See yourself through yourself without any emotion.

Preksha Dhyan is a practice to see the soul through the soul. Meditate to see yourself. Resolve to meditate:

I am practising Preksha Dhyan to cleanse my mind (repeat to yourself).

Adopt the mudra of *kayotsarga*.

All parts of the body should be still like a sculpture. Relax and concentrate. Concentrate on the right toe, suggest it to relax and observe it relaxing. Similarly, see every part of the body, suggest its relaxation and experience the relaxation. And practise being still.

Begin *chaitanya-kendra* practice.

Focus on the navel. See the entire region in a straight line to the *sushumna* (the channel that runs along the spinal cord in the centre, through the seven chakras).

Experience all the vibrations in the region. Be alert. See the entire region.

Concentrate.

Now observe the *ananda kendra*. In the depression between the ribs, near the heart, take the mind along in a straight line, like the light from a torch. Go up to the back. Slow your breathing. Deepen concentration. Experience the vibrations in the region.

Now move to the *vishuddhi kendra*—the space in the centre of the throat. Concentrate. Take the light of the mind through the entire region. Experience the vibrations of the breath. In full and deep concentration. Slow your breathing. Concentrate for two minutes at every point.

Now move to the front portion of the tongue. Let the tongue not touch the palate or the inner cheeks. Let it be free. Concentrate on its front portion. Experience the vibrations of the breath.

Next, focus on the tip of the nose and experience the vibrations there.

Focus on the right ear, inside, outside, around it and experience the vibrations. Focus on the centre for rectitude.

Repeat with the left ear.

Focus on the right eye—the window into the head. Look deep within it and experience the vibrations.

Repeat with the left eye.

Focus on the *darshana kendra*—the space between the two eyes and eyebrows. Concentrate on that space and take the light of the mind right to the back of the head. Experience the vibrations. Slow your breathing.

Search for truth in oneself.

Practice amity with all.

For liberation from sorrow, pursue right knowledge and right conduct.

Recite:

Arham te saranam pavajjami
Siddhe saranam pavajjami
Sahu saranam pavajjami
Kevalipannatam dhammam saranam pavajjami

Preksha practice complete.

Perception of psychic colours

The principle of *leshya* has two aspects: feeling and colour. Colours have a great impact on our minds—not only do they influence the state of mind, they also help change it.

In the malevolent class,

i. The most intense are *krishna*—dark black.
ii. The medium ones are *nila*—blue dark.
iii. The least intense ones are *kapota*—grey.

Similarly, in the benevolent class,

i. The least intense ones are *tejas*—bright red.
ii. The medium ones are *padma*—bright yellow.
iii. The most intense ones are *shukla*—bright white.

When one is under the influence of the evil trinity of *krishna*, *nila* and *kapota*, the instinctive drive is so powerful that the reasoning mind surrenders to it. On the other hand, with the conversion of *leshyas*, the rational mind is able to countermand the carnal desires.

Colour is an inherent characteristic of the entire material existence. Colours are produced by visible light which is a form of electromagnetic radiation. The differences in wavelength and frequency distinguish one colour from another. Different *leshyas* have different wavelengths, each having a definite place in the electromagnetic spectrum. Each one, therefore, can be associated through its harmonics with a definite colour in the visible spectrum, that is from red to violet. Thus, based on the relation between the colours of the visible spectrum and the *leshya* radiations, we can use specific colours as the means of strengthening or weakening the *leshya* radiations.

The spiritual progress will depend upon the degree of transformation of the malevolent trinity into the benevolent one. Without actual transformation, there will be no progress. This is not merely a speculation, but the basis of a real experience. And to bring about the desired transformation, the perception of psychic colour, or *leshya dhyana,* has proved to be a practical means of transformation. *Leshya dhyana* is thus an efficient tool of successively diminishing the intensities of the malevolent *leshya*—from *krishna* to *nila* and from *nila* to *kapota*, and then progressively increasing the intensities of the benevolent *leshya*—from *tejas* to *padma* and from *padma* to *shukla*. The actual spiritual progress commences with the conversion of *kapota* to *tejas*, that is, from grey to red. The index of *tejas leshya* is the bright red colour of the sunrise. Colour psychology also supports the view that the bright red colour is the first indication of spiritual progress.

With the above conversion, there is a remarkable drop in animal instincts and carnal desires and other bad habits. Further progress will result from the change of *tejas leshya* to *padma leshya* and the final change of *padma leshya* to *shukla leshya* will result in the total eradication of cruelty and hatred.

The aura

It is now known that the body is always surrounded by an array of colours called 'aura', which is, in effect, *leshya*. Change in *leshya* will bring about a corresponding change in the colour of aura. That is why our aura is governed at different times by different colours such as black, red, yellow, blue or white.

Aura is not only influenced by the internal colour indices but also the colours of the external environment. That is why the cause-and-effect relation between *leshya* and colours is reciprocal. In other words, just as a change in *leshya* would result in a change in the colour of our aura, a change in aura due to the influence of the colours of the external environment would bring about a change in the *leshya*. This principle has been utilized in the perception of the psychic colours (*leshya dhyana*) to transform the malevolent *leshya* into benevolent ones.

Meditation and contemplation

Preksha Dhyan focuses on perception, that is, to perceive without attachment or aversion, excluding thoughts of the past or imaginations of the future.

Contemplation is what occurs after we have engaged in *preksha*, or deep and profound perception. In this way, Preksha Dhyan is a complete system of spiritual development, involving meditation on both perception and contemplation. Perception is used as the first technique of meditation, whereas in the later technique the mind is encouraged to concentrate on the thought process, or contemplation.

In brief, Preksha Dhyan is of two kinds:

- Concentration of perception known as *preksha*.
- Concentration of thoughts known as *anupreksha*.

It is stated in the *Dhyan Shatak* that at the end of each meditation session, contemplation must be performed. After meditation, four contemplations are generally practised:

- Solitariness
- Transitoriness
- Tolerance
- Amity

Objectives

Profound perception is an extremely valuable technique for acquainting oneself with the facets of life. However, in order to change one's habits, one must undertake the path of contemplation. It is an art of giving suggestions. A person can make suggestions either to himself (autosuggestion) or he can accept suggestions dictated by someone else. If suggestions are repeated over a period, they get registered in our subconscious and translate into habits.

The main objectives of contemplation are:

- To change one's character or habit by registering a resolution in the subconscious mind.
- To realize the eternal truth through deep mental concentration.
- To develop virtues leading to emotional transformation.
- To eradicate psychological disorders, especially phobias.

Benefits

Contemplation is a technique by which positive transformation of negative emotions, such as disgust, jealousy, fear and aversion, can be achieved. The other benefits include:

(a) Physical

- Strengthens the immune system.
- Brings desirable physical changes.
- Relieves body aches.

(b) Psychological

- Replaces negative thoughts with positive ones.
- Enhances mental abilities.
- Improves imagination.
- Imparts good decision-making power.

(c) Emotional

- Transforms attitude and behaviour.
- Rectifies negative instincts and replaces them with positive ones.
- Enables attainment of happiness.
- Facilitates a cool temperament.

(d) Spiritual

- Inculcates spiritual doctrines in the subconscious.
- Converts materialistic outlook into a spiritual one.
- Enables realization of the truth.

In brief, contemplation can be practised to change deep-rooted habits and addictions, including drinking, smoking, stealing and lying. Contemplation of any reverse determination that we communicate to our subconscious mind can prove very effective under such situations.

Mantra meditation

In Sanskrit, the word 'mantra' means a liberator of mind. A mantra is composed of potent sound syllables that are capable of influencing the human system both physically and spiritually.

Many seed letters and terms or phrases that can be recited incantatory are available for chanting. Among these, 'aum', 'hreem', 'shreem' and 'kleem' are seed letters. These are invested with great powers. An articulation of a word generates a special kind of soundwaves and vibrations, which influence our mind.

Mantra plays an important role in Preksha Dhyan.

Why should we practise mantra meditation?

- The human mind is inherently unstable. It does not concentrate on one point for a long time. The chanting of mantra is an easy and effective tool for focussing the mind on one object and achieving better concentrations.
- Mantras help break our unconscious and subconscious thoughts and desire patterns, which bind us to past conditioning. The seed mantra is a thought force and generates energy. Our subconscious is restructured by the energy of the mantra.
- Mantras can create a protective shield for a practitioner, which helps him to pursue meditation for longer durations.
- Mantras are an important tool for clearing and cleansing the mind.
- They enable the development of inner power.
- Mantras are a source for self-purification.

How does it work?

- The vibrations of sound produced by a person influences both the person and the space. When a practitioner pronounces a mantra, the vibration of sound influences the gross body, especially the spinal cord and the neurons. The intensity of the sound vibrations increases, influencing the subtle body. This way, through mantra meditation, one gets rid of diseases, brings transformation in behaviour and attitude, and develops inner power.

- The sound vibrations get amplified with the help of vital energy and the strength of the practitioner's consciousness, increasing the frequency of soundwaves far beyond the limits of ultrasonic and supersonic vibrations.
- The human brain is made up of interconnected neurons. When we think, each neuron forms a strong path known as memory. When we read a book several times, we remember most of the topics and can recall them because we strengthen these pathways and create memories. When a mantra is chanted several times, it strengthens certain pathways, giving us certain mental powers depending on our need and aptitude.

Technique

- The chanting of mantras is of three types, characterized by high-voiced, low-voiced and silent chanting, which are classified as
    - Chanting
    - Low-toned chanting
    - Chanting mentally
- The process constitutes an effort to migrate from the gross to the subtle. Gross sounds produce gross vibrations and subtle sounds produce subtle vibrations. Subtle vibrations are far more powerful than the gross ones.
- In the initial stages, in bringing about a change, gross vibrations play a key role. However, in order to achieve higher levels of change, and in advanced stages of

meditation, it is essential to be able to move towards the subtle vibrations. In the subtle stages, the distance between the meaning and the words disappear. At this stage, language and thought come closer to each other and become indistinguishable.

- To have better concentration during mantra meditation, various psychic centres are used. Along with them, colours are also used.
- We can also synchronize our breath with mantra meditation.

Precautions

For the chanting of mantra to be effective and fruitful, it is essential that recitation be done diligently and systematically in a correct manner. Wrong pronunciation of words, lack of concentration during chanting, and too fast or too lethargically performed chanting are some of the major obstacles in realizing the benefits of this technique.

Sample mantra recitation

There are a number of mantras that have been successfully applied during Preksha Dhyan training programmes. 'Arham' and 'Aum Hreem Arham Namah' are commonly used.

The technique of reciting the latter is as follows:

- While reciting the word 'Aum', concentrate on the tip of the nose, the centre of vital energy. Try to perceive the mantra on this centre.

- Shift your attention to the middle of the eyebrows, the centre of intuition, and perceive the mantra 'Hreem' there.
- Now focus your total attention on the middle of the forehead, the centre of enlightenment, and visualize the mantra 'Arham'.
- Towards the end, concentrate on the front of the head, the centre of peace, and perceive the mantra 'Namah' here.

In the first stage, recite the mantra. In the next stage, realize the mantra on the specific centre with bright white colour. At this stage, mantra becomes meditation.

Benefits

- Improves concentration.
- Cures diseases if used with the right technique.
- Brings transformation in behaviour and habits.
- Increases inner power.

Specific mantras have specific benefits associated with them.

A few examples are given below with a word of caution: mantras have to be recited with mental calm and complete concentration. Their pronunciation should be right.

To realize one's imagined goal

The following mantra is to be recited 108 times a day: *Om Hrim Shrim Arham O si aa oo sa namaha.*

Totally, the number of repetitions should be 1.25 lakh times.

Result: the imagined goal becomes a reality. We have already discussed in the book that the goal should be within the laws that govern human life. Mental peace also comes with the recitation of this mantra.

To recite when facing difficulty

The following mantra is to be recited 108 times a day: *Om Hrim lom Nnamo loye savva sahunnam.*

Result: mitigates problems.

Before undertaking the recitation of a mantra, one should visualize the desired end. The second step is to decide to access the desired end. The third step is to take action towards the end. These three steps constitute the process of autosuggestion. The mantras may be recited loud or softly, preferably in silence and solitude.

The effects of all the different exercises mentioned above depend on the capability and aptitude of the practitioner. Padma Shri Dr S.C. Manchanda, ex-head of cardiology at All India Institute of Medical Sciences, Delhi has been propagating Preksha Dhyan for more than thirty years as a medical practitioner. In fact, he is the one who has carried out scientific studies establishing the efficacy of Preksha meditation in dealing with and reversing cardiac blockages.

So, if the physical heart can be brought under control, the mind cannot be too far behind.

Part 3

Acharya Mahapragya: The Light from Within

By Sudhamahi Regunathan

When Acharya Mahapragya told Dr A.P.J. Abdul Kalam, former President who had played a key role in Pokhran-II and was also known as the Missile Man of India, 'What we need is a second type of atom bomb that can diffuse or deactivate the deadly atom bomb, which spreads the radiance of peace all over,' he was justifiably surprised. 'A unique concept,' he exclaimed. The acharya narrated a mythological story to illustrate his point: 'Vaishyayan was an immature ascetic. He had the gift of fire power. He indiscriminately used his power to kill. Mahavira saw this destructive use of power and immediately used a counter spell to extinguish that fire completely.'

In this strange coming together of science and spirituality, Acharya Mahapragya defined himself. The bridge he built between the two rested on some of his strongest convictions.

Foremost among them was his belief that nothing was impossible, though it could appear so. Just because we are not able to see something, we cannot deny its existence. He placed equal importance on both the gross and the subtle worlds. He suggested that we should not go by just what is manifest and should also consider and explore the unmanifest.

When the lightning
Concealed within the haven of the cloud
Drew the line of light
Then one came to know
That 'is' comes from 'is not'
The definition of existence
The eternal union of
form and negation.

The idea of the unmanifest branches into two underlying presumptions. Firstly, that there is more than the manifest, thus admitting to the existence of the subtle world. The subtle world, the world which escapes the eyes, the world that exists but can only be, at best, experienced, contains secrets that need to be understood. If an idea can come to us, that means it can manifest in some way. Secondly, the idea of the unmanifest suggests that both the manifest and the unmanifest exist together.

This brings us to the second great conviction that Acharya Mahapragya built his life on. He had complete faith in the relativity of truth, or the philosophical concept of anekanta. He firmly believed in the Jaina principle that the entire truth cannot be captured in words and so all that we speak of as truth is but a part of it. He expanded this idea further to declare opposites coexist. Darkness and light, sun and shade, sweetness and bitterness and so on. That brought him great acceptance of people and thoughts, which were diverse and even contradictory. When he formed the Foundation for Understanding Religions and Enlightened Citizenship, he said, 'If truths from all the religions were to come together, maybe we will get closer to the absolute truth.'

His third conviction was that true development can happen only when it is imbued with compassion. Scientific growth should hold empathy as one of its principles for the direction of progress. On reflection, every human endeavour is focussed towards gaining a better understanding of life. Within the gamut of ideas that engulf human life, there also lies its relationship with the animate and inanimate world, in addition to eternal questions, such as how did life come to be, is there life anywhere else in this universe, how does it function, what is afterlife, if there is one and so on. Even though we have understood much, we still have a long way to go. To imbue this understanding with concern has come to be known as compassion. One of the characterizing features of humans is believed to be their ability to think and feel—and that is how the emotion of compassion is born. Compassion has been highlighted time and again as the most valued quality of humanity and humaneness. It extends to all living beings and is born out of the overarching guide to life: ahimsa.

Acharya Mahapragya lived by ahimsa so intensely that he considered it violence even to give a verbal order or assert an opinion. All he did was suggest. Progress, be it in science or individual life, should stand the test of ahimsa. He looked at ahimsa as diplomacy, as poetry, as art. He saw ahimsa as the essence of moral values. He saw ahimsa as the art of living life. So much so that when he was awarded the Indira Gandhi Communal Harmony Award he was surprised and said, 'I wonder why my name has been selected for the award. The selectors are notable personalities, so I am not questioning their judgement. But I still wonder because ahimsa is the sole religion of my life and communal harmony is but a flower of this bush of roses. If I can spread the fragrance, then where is the need for the award?'

In his play, *Ratnapalacharitam*, there is a dialogue when the night is accused of being evil, for it is the night which encourages and provides cover for the evil that takes place. This idea resonates the association of darkness with ignorance and light with illumination or enlightenment. Night says, 'The evil lies not within me. It is the darkness within you that makes you perform the evil acts.' So, he plays with ideas and similes to highlight the need for ahimsa.

However, it still remains a mystery as to how to develop the attitude of ahimsa, why it does not find mass appeal, what makes a non-violent attitude and so on. The story of Acharya Mahapragya's life is the story of attempts to improve this understanding. They range from his study of diverse cultures and ideas, his own experiments with meditative practices and their reflection in his writings. Acharya Mahapragya believed words alone do not lend experience. Practice is essential—just as morally upright conduct alone reflects learning, not words or qualifications. Therefore, just as we build and develop the intellect, we must nurture and shape a person's character. He culled out essentials from traditional techniques of meditation to present a comprehensive and complete system called Preksha Dhyan. Beyond logic and the mind, if some traits have to be changed, if some qualities have to be developed in order to improve conduct, Acharya Mahapragya said that we would have to look into ourselves. He believed that everyone could better themselves and conquer negative emotions. The inner world has as many adventures to offer, in fact, more than the outer world can ever hold. To get in touch with the soul would mean to obliterate all barriers between the inner self and the outer world. The duality will merge into oneness of being and then knowledge and the knower would be one. It is at that level that true creativity finds expression. True power of the self can be uncovered. This is his fourth conviction.

Acharya Mahapragya was the tenth spiritual head of the Jaina Svetambara Terapanth community. They are a community who follow the teachings of Mahavira, as all Jains do. Vardhamana Mahavira was the twenty-fourth Tirthankara of the Jainas. He belonged to the sixth century BCE and the Jainas trace a long mythological history before him. The community is sharply divided between ascetics who live a life of renunciation and householders who are their followers. The monks and nuns have an acharya, the head in spiritual matters, not only of the ascetics but of the entire community. Acharya Mahapragya was one such community head. A head who had not a penny to his name held the responsibility of showing the right path, right thinking and right action to some of the highest taxpayers and richest members of society.

Mahapragya is his acquired name, a name his guru, Acharya Tulsi, anointed him with when he identified him as his successor. His parents had named him Nathmal, or the precious one. And he was precious, not just as every child is to the parents but because he was the son born after two daughters, and that too after a long gap. Back in the day, in society, and that too in the conservative heart of Rajasthan, the birth of a son was considered to be the highest blessing, as Acharya Mahapragya himself comments rather wryly in his autobiography. The father, Tolaram, full of joy and pride at the birth of his son, seemed to have known his end was close, for he had told his wife that she would have a son, but would be widowed. And so it happened when Nathmal was but two and a half months old.

Nathmal's elder sisters got married and went to their husbands' villages. Nathmal and his mother lived in the dusty, remote village of Tamkor. As Acharya Mahapragya writes, 'An entirely rural setting. Neither roads nor railway tracks. No car, bus or even trucks. No one had heard of petrol and the fumes emanating from a petrol-run vehicle had not settled in anyone's eyes. Only two means of transport ... bullock cart and the camel. There were many wells, but the water was brackish. Drinking water was scarce. There was no school in Tamkor. In that village I was born.'

He was born on 14 July 1920. He lived a pampered life even though he lost his father at a young age. His father's brothers, his mother and his sisters doted over him. He lost one of his cousins when he was seven or eight. The cousin, who was much older to him, had been very fond of him and his loss was felt greatly by Nathmal Choraria.

In a sense, Nathmal seemed to have the life of any other child. He went on holidays, particularly to his sisters' homes. He had a few possessions that he was very proud of and were the envy of his peers. He played a lot and was curious. Somehow and over time, life veered him towards monkhood. His mother was religious, so, perhaps, that became the immediate reason. At the age of ten, he was initiated into a life of renunciation. As he says, 'I cannot give any of the standard answers people give when asked why they got initiated. They say, the world seemed bereft of excitement and so they became monks. Or that afraid of the cycle of birth and death, they became monks. Or even that in the fear of hell and in the desire of heaven, they became monks. I like to give only one answer to this—the one that I have been giving all along: it was some unknown inspiration which caused this event to occur in the world known to us.' The interesting part is that not only did he join the Terapanth fold, he insisted that his mother, who too sought renunciation, be permitted along with him. Once initiated, their worldly relationship ceased to matter as their identity as a monk and a nun took precedence.

Life as a monk is not easy, but Nathmal got so much love and care from his seniors in his fold that he felt cared for and encouraged. He noted, 'If a child gets to grow in an environment of love, all his innate qualities get nourishment and he blossoms. Constant reprimand makes a child cringe and an environment of love makes the child develop. The environment of reprimand is a helpless condition created under duress. Love is our natural state. With love and the right nourishment, even plants blossom. What then to say of human beings? I got very little reprimands and more love, so I was lucky to find the important and right stimulus to development.'

His eighty years of monkhood were not without personal challenges. When he was still a teenager, his eyes gave him trouble. He could not read, and his eyes watered all the time. He himself recounted that it was a depressing time, for he thought he would never read or write again. But the right treatment and providence cured it within a few months. In that period, however, he decided not to get left behind in his studies and started learning by heart the texts he had read earlier. This gave him an edge over his peers. Having never been to a school, young Nathmal did not know how to learn or the importance of learning. His handwriting was also not well-formed. But he resolved that he would be second to none, and with sheer dint of practice and hard work, came to be recognized as the repository of wisdom and knowledge. And that is how he got the name 'Mahapragya'.

As a child monk, he was mischievous. He and his peers would burst into laughter easily and frequently. They would chatter and play games when their teacher, Acharya Tulsi, was not present; as soon as they heard him coming, they would fall silent and get back to their books. And they were competitive. They each wanted to study better than the other, to earn the teacher's approval. It may help us better understand, with the right education, that which created a great mind with a rare clarity of thought and power of compassion, if we are able to identify the element which worked despite the normalcy of growing up, albeit in a hostel-like atmosphere that emphasized discipline and moral rectitude.

Through the eighty-year period, Muni Nathmal studied various Indian philosophies, Western scholars and of course the Jaina Agamas. His position as a monk kept him in meditative solitude and yet brought him in contact with different kinds of people. Some with deep piety, some in positions of power, some scholars and some practitioners from different faiths.

His position as an acharya, and earlier as Yuvacharya, the successor to the Acharya Tulsi, brought him administrative knowledge and experience. The head of the spiritual sangha is the spiritual mentor of many organizations within the fold, involving managing matters pertaining to the community as a whole and the ascetics as a separate group. The organizations range from those committed to social service to even a university. The network of these organizations is spread all over India and abroad. His is a story of solitude and isolation in the midst of a multitude in the throes of change. A major event in his life was India's independence from British rule. We find he has explored the idea of independence in detail and written extensively on the responsibility that comes with true freedom. Smaller, but no less significant, changes were many, including social reform movements at many levels. The desire for equality was at the crux of social reformation and that is the reason, perhaps, why Acharya Mahapragya, after appreciating the theory of socialism and finding it impractical in practice, turned to anekanta for a solution.

> That which emerged from wisdom
> Is the truth.
> That which derived from research
> Is the principle.

Acharya Mahapragya felt communist philosophy kept religion out of its ambit and was therefore incomplete and unsuccessful in bringing about transformation. The desire for equality amongst all living beings, not just humans, is the thrust of Jaina philosophy. But at its core lay not the principles of communism but the findings of anekanta, which accept differences and similarities as expressions of the same essence, the core, of absolute truth. Acharya Mahapragya could never agree with one socialistic contention—that to achieve a lofty goal unfair means may be adopted. He writes, 'Acharya Bhikshu's [the founder of the Terapanth community] principle of fair means towards fair goals was imprinted in my mind. Those days Gandhiji's views were discussed a lot. He too was emphasizing the need for fair means towards a fair end. Few thinkers have emphasized this principle as much as Gandhiji did in the field of politics and Acharya Bhikshu in the field of philosophy.'

The process of change hurtled on at great speed to the complete opening up of economy with globalization. Acharya Mahapragya must have felt the pulse of this change intensely, for the community that nurtured and nourished him were traders and businessmen. He responded to this economic stimulus by making a difference between need and want. Wants are unlimited. Needs are limited. The needs of every being can be fulfilled. And that should be the target, he declared, bringing the idea of *aparigraha,* or non-possession, to the fore. This is an important philosophical idea of Jaina thought. It suggests that limiting wants, or limiting possessiveness, however it is viewed. Acharya Mahapragya thus interpreted a complicated philosophy in a manner relevant to the ordinary man.

Capturing the repetitive humdrum of ordinary life, negating none of the material impulses or compulsions, Acharya Mahapragya captured the essence of human existence in his sermons and writings. His writings have an aphoristic quality and since they contain fragments of eternal truth, they continue to ring true long after they have been penned.

As Muni Nathmal, he found his interest in literature was next only to his interest in philosophy. In his early twenties, he became a published writer and wrote in Sanskrit, Prakrit and Hindi, as well as Rajasthani. Some telling verses come to mind:

Hope
The only definition
Of life.

And,

To come too close
To too bright a light
Is not good
To say this
The stars of the day
Are very eager
But the light of the sun
Even for two seconds
Is not willing to unveil them.

His style of writing is reflective of his way of life: one of restraint. This could be the reason why he has many poetic works to his credit. Perhaps because brevity captures the essence of perfection, it is all that we can take in of perfection. Though his writing resonates with even those who do not know the Jaina texts, to those who know them, the inspiration and the context lend them more depth and dimension. For example, a poem of his reads:

The nest among the intertwined branches
Of a neem tree
Revealed …
There is not just love in the birds
There is wisdom too.
The leaves of the neem tree
Were rustling
The sparrow in the nest was
Still, peaceful and undisturbed.

The poem just seems to say the wise sparrow chose a safe spot to build her nest so that it does not sway with the wind and her loved ones are secure. In terms of philosophy, this poem refers to the idea of anekanta bringing together the opposites of movement and stillness. It also extols the virtue of stillness, both of the mind and the body, as we have seen in the practice of meditation. In that stillness, peace and calm are perceived.

As he wrote:

That which words spoke
Flowed away
That which silence said
Remained.

Between expression, movement, thought, silence, pause and emptiness, there has always been the quest for truth, the quest for the beautiful, the quest for the eternal. And this was what Acharya Mahapragya was seeking.

A Note on Sources

This book has been prepared from articles, essays and sermons of Acharya Mahapragya. The introduction to every chapter has been written by his translator Sudhamahi Regunathan

The first chapter is from his autobiography, *Yatra Ek Akinchan Ki*, published by Jain Vishva Bharati, Ladnun (2010), where he recounts how he aspired to be second to none. His main motivation was that he should not let his guru down. So he actively sought success; a success that was built on maximizing his potential, with industry and humility. He faced many challenges: as a student he had problems with his eyesight and so could not read for long durations. He used this time to learn by heart the Jaina texts. This gave him an advantage over his peers in later years. When his health was weak, he delved into Ayurveda to learn the right foods that can build the right climate within the body for good health. He pursued knowledge with devotion till he realized that knowledge without practice was not complete. Thus, he devised the system of meditation called Preksha Dhyan.

The second chapter is the essence of the paragraph above: how he overcame challenges with positivity. Acharya

Mahapragya held that it was important to think the right thoughts and this chapter is drawn from the book, *The Art of Positive Thinking*, published by B. Jain Publishers Pvt Ltd in 1994.

The second chapter lays the foundation for the third chapter, which is again culled from his autobiography where he pens down his sutras to success. These are the sutras he followed in life.

The fourth chapter is from a book called *The Quest for Truth*: *In the Context of Anekanta*, published by Jain Vishva Bharati Institute (2003). Acharya Mahapragya wrote a trilogy on anekanta. The first is, *Anekanta, Tisra Netra* and the fifth chapter of this book is derived from its translation, *Anekanta, the Third Eye*, by Sudhamahi Regunathan and published by Jain Vishva Bharati Institute, Ladnun (2002). The second is *The Quest for Truth*: *In the Context of Anekanta*. And the third is *Anekanta and Jain Philosophy*. All these books were an attempt to demystify the philosophical concept of anekanta to make it applicable to and practical in everyday life. Another book, *Anekanta: The Philosophy of Coexistence*, explains the concept in a simple manner. Chapter 6, which presents the philosophical basis of anekanta for readers who wonder on the scope of a seemingly simple idea, is from this book.

Acharya Mahapragya has always placed great importance to the way of thinking. *The Art of Positive Thinking* devotes two chapters on how to gain freedom from reaction. Chapter 7 has been extracted from there.

One of his books which has been translated many times, under different titles and continues to be relevant, is the one originally titled *Main Mera Man aur Meri Shanti* (translation: Me, My Mind and My Peace). One of its early translations, by Prof. R.P. Bhatnagar and published by Jain Vishva Bharati Institute in 1995, is titled *I and Mine*. It has also been subsequently translated under the title, *Ramblings of an Ascetic*. The ideal title should perhaps lie somewhere between the two. Chapter 8 is from this book. Chapters 17 and 18 are also from it.

Chapters 9 and 10 are drawn from *Mind Beyond Mind*, a book which examines the mind and how it can be brought under control, made stable and focussed.

One of Acharya Mahapragya's pet ideas was that a society can be healthy only when a man is healthy; health here refers not just to physical health but also to mental health. *New Man, New World* talks of a new world order that can be created if the human being learns how to conduct and nurture himself. Chapters 11–15 draw from this book published by Adarsh Sahitya Sangh, New Delhi.

Chapter 2 is from Acharya Mahapragya's book, *Economics of Mahavira*. His practicality is seen in the fact that he does not talk of greatness and fame by ignoring the impact of economics in our life. The question is, how to manage both types of demand so that we can lead a balanced life, more fulfilled than the one portrayed by materialism alone.

From *Philosophical Foundations of Jainism*, published by Adarsha Sahitya Sangha, New Delhi, the first chapter in the second section explains the basic tenets of Jainism. The chapter on Preksha Dhyan is culled from *The Mirror of The Self* and from a little monograph titled *Science of Living*.

Many of the short stories that have been used to illustrate ideas are from the three volumes of *Mahapragya ki Kathayen*.

Acharya Mahapragya has written many books of poetry. Some poems are from *The Sun Will Rise Again*, published by Penguin (2008) and translated by Sudhamahi Regunathan; while the rest are from the compilation titled *The Sound of Silence*, translated by Sudhamahi Regunathan and Samani Chaitanyapragya, published by Jain Vishva Bharati Institute, in 2005.

Index

Translator's Acknowledgements

Acharya Mahapragya's birth centenary celebrations began in June of 2019 when he would have entered his hundredth year had he been alive. (He passed on in 2010.)

It was at the commencement of the centenary year that Surendra Patawari (Belgium-Momasar) got the idea that Acharya-ji's teachings should be collated and made available to readers outside the community. He contacted me through Rajendra Sancheti who was also excited about the project. Surendra Choraria, on whom Acharya Mahapragya had always reposed a lot of confidence, endorsed the idea. The selection of material provided by them to be used for this compilation greatly help in shaping the book. M.L. Sethia and Dr Y.S. Rajan shared the enthusiasm and, as always, I drew a lot from them.

My special thanks to K.C. Jain, currently Director, Adhyatma Sadhna Kendra, Mehrauli, Delhi for giving me information about Preksha Dhyan. Regular Preksha camps are held in Adhyatma Sadhna Kendra. My gratitude to my friend Shriti Nath, who, as usual, gave valuable comments.

My gratitude also to Krishan Chopra for believing in the book and to my editor Suchismita Ukil for making the book deserving of it. I am grateful to Anita Sharma for her clarity and support. Amit Malhotra's creativity has led me to say, go by the book cover!

The book speaks of interdependence. In that spirit I have so many to thank. To all of them and to my family, my immeasurable gratitude. To my husband, who also enjoyed Acharya Maharpagya's confidence, I have a special word of gratitude for his patient listening and meaningful suggestions.

About the Author

Acharya Mahapragya was the tenth spiritual guru of the Jaina Swetambar Terapanth community (15 June–9 May 2010). He became a monk at the age of ten and lived to a month short of ninety years. Through the eighty year period, Acharya Mahapragya studied vastly: Indian philosophies, Western scholars and of course the Jaina agamas. His position as a monk kept him in meditative solitude. His position as the leader of the community brought him into contact with different kinds of people, some in deep piety, some in total disregard, some scholars and some practitioners from different faiths. This resulted in a study of human nature which evolved into not just a customized method of meditation, Preksha Dhyan, but also helped understand how to develop the human potential to its ultimate.

He has authored over 300 books, including *The Mysteries of Mind* (1982), *The Art of Positive Thinking* (2002) and *The Family and the Nation* (2008).